EYEWITNESS

THE TRUE STORY OF THE NORTHPORT AZTAKEA WOODS MURDER

BY

ALBERT QUINONES

Copyright © 2023 Albert Quinones
All rights reserved
First Edition

NEWMAN SPRINGS PUBLISHING
320 Broad Street
Red Bank, NJ 07701

First originally published by Newman Springs Publishing 2023

ISBN 978-1-63881-972-1 (Paperback)
ISBN 978-1-63881-973-8 (Digital)

Printed in the United States of America

I'm dedicating this book to Elizabeth. If it weren't for her, this book would not have been written. She was my everything and I loved her more than anything in this world. I let her go to write this book. I didn't chase her because I loved her that much. I didn't want to see her go through the shit show that I'm going through now to write this book for everyone. There was only one word that explained what we were, and that was love. So, I dedicate this book to Elizabeth, my everything. Thank you for helping me get the courage to do this. Just know, Elizabeth, you are my all.

AUTHOR'S NOTE

THE STORIES YOU were about to read are true. I have changed only one name to protect the identity of one person. All of the people that you will be reading about are the original people who had, in some way, shape or form or some involvement in this story. The people that were interviewed stated to me—the author—that they have not interviewed with anyone other than me—the author—within thirty-eight years.

This book is to debunk the lies and myths that have been going on for way too long and put the facts out there once and for all.

The stories are original stories and facts of their encounters of what happened in 1984 of July—over a hundred hours of recorded interview.

So I hope this book brings closure and peace and helps people get through the hard times that they encounter in their lives. Then it was worth writing this book.

CONTENTS

Let the Truth Be Known at Last ix
Marketing Eyewitness xiii
Preface xv

Chapter 1: Let the Truth Be Known 1
Chapter 2: Who We Were 11
Chapter 3: The Day It Happened 23
Chapter 4: Rolling Stones 47
Chapter 5: Sarah—Ricky Kasso's Girlfriend 58
Chapter 6: William Leason—Interview One 69
Chapter 7: William Leason—Interview Two 81
Chapter 8: Robert Atkinson 90
Chapter 9: Richard Barton 96

Chapter 10: Mark Florimonte............................111
Chapter 11: Karen Novellino—Jimmy's
             Girlfriend...119
Chapter 12: Character and Credibility of
             Robert Howard (Northport
             Chief of Police) 127
Chapter 13: Closure..134

Conclusion...233
Sources..237
Acknowledgments 239

LET THE TRUTH BE KNOWN AT LAST
JUNE 16, 1984

ONLY FOUR PEOPLE know what happened in the Aztakea Woods in Northport, New York, on June 16, 1984. That night, sixteen-year-old Ricky Kasso murdered his friend Gary Lauwers in Aztakea Woods. Albert Quinones and Jimmy Troiano witnessed the crime. After his arrest on July 4, Kasso hung himself in his jail cell.

Jimmy Troiano was arrested and charged with second-degree murder; with only one remaining eyewitness, the case against him hung on Albert

Quinones's testimony. The local police pressured him to assert that Troiano had assisted in the murder. He was a scared child with no one to turn to, and at first, he told the authorities the truth, but they did not want to hear it and wanted me to lie. But at trial, he told the truth, and Jimmy Troiano was acquitted.

The Gary Lauwers murder was shocking in its violence. He was stabbed over one hundred fifty times, his eyes were stabbed out of his face, and a thrill-hungry fake news media jumped on the story. Reporters camped out in front of Jimmy Troiano's and Albert Quinones's homes, harassing their families and neighbors in their small suburban town. A "true crime" book, *Say You Love Satan*, was published in 1987, but it was more fiction than fact, and so much of what was true was plagiarized.

Now for the first time, Albert Quinones will tell the true story of the Northport Aztakea Woods murder, and much more, in *Eyewitness: The True Story of the Northport Aztakea Woods Murder*. Albert Quinones will reveal what actually happened that night and describe the familial, cultural, and socio-economic environment that turned him and his friends—and an entire generation of kids—toward alcohol, drugs, heavy metal music, and ultimately, violence. He will also tell the story of his life in the thirty-eight years since, including his career in the military and his struggles to leave drugs and his past behind him.

The murder of Gary Lauwers was a tragedy borne out of a dispute between two troubled teenagers. In Quinones's view, it was the inevitable result of an environment of parental neglect and/or abuse, part and parcel of 1970s-style social permissiveness lingering into the early 1980s. But in Ronald Reagan's America, religious conservatism was a rising political force, and governmental authorities and law enforcement saw Satan everywhere. Between preachers calling for the burning of heavy metal albums, the belief in "recovered memories" that led to hysterical prosecutions of day care workers, and other factors, people wanted to believe that there was something evil at work; they needed a monster, so they created one in Ricky Kasso.

In *Eyewitness: The True Story of the Northport Aztakea Woods Murder*, Albert Quinones will tell the world who Ricky Kasso, Jimmy Troiano, and Gary Lauwers really were; he will describe how a terrible tragedy was turned into a sensationalized, fabricated narrative by greedy and cynical tabloids and local news reporters; he will reveal the pressure put on him by legal authorities seeking a quick victory in court, the truth be damned; and he will describe the impact all of these events had on his life, as a troubled teenager and a traumatized adult. Ultimately, this is a story of hope.

While Ricky Kasso and Gary Lauwers are dead and Jimmy Troiano is in prison on an unrelated charge, Albert Quinones has come out of this ordeal as highly decorated combat engineer veteran of the United States Army, a self-made success in the construction industry, and a loyal friend and family man.

MARKETING EYEWITNESS

INTEREST IN TRUE crime stories is at an all-time high at the moment. The *Serial* podcast created a sensation in 2014, and more recently, the Netflix series *Making a Murderer* and Michelle McNamara's book *I'll Be Gone in the Dark* were both wildly popular. In the latter case, the author's research led to the arrest of a serial killer who had been evading capture for decades.

Other books, like Kier-La Janisse and Paul Corupe's *Satanic Panic: Pop-Cultural Paranoia in the 1980s* and Richard Beck's *We Believe the Children: A Moral Panic in the 1980s*, have created a strong interest in looking back at the era Albert Quinones will be discussing. His ability to debunk the myths that have arisen over the last three decades plus surrounding the Northport Aztakea Woods murder will make this book a unique entry into the marketplace, and one sure to attract interest from true crime aficionados, people with long pop culture memories, metal fans, and perhaps most importantly, people who have been victims of trauma or have come out of long-term drug dependencies, who can take inspiration from Albert Quinones's journey toward a better life.

PREFACE

AS SOON AS I returned to Northport, the memories came rushing back. It's been so long. The snapshots flash across my mind, taking me back to my younger years. Here's me and my friends Ricky Kasso and Gary Lauwers going to elementary school together, riding our bikes, hanging out at the park—there were concerts there every weekend. The memories keep racing forward, one after another, like the water splashing against the Northport Harbor docks.

The good memories inevitably make way for the bad memories, the ones that have been haunting me ever since Ricky killed Gary in June 1984. I might as well have died a little bit too that night. The feelings I've carried across these decades—the shame and guilt and sadness and second-guessing, wondering if I could have done something to help Gary—along with the horrible nightmares… I don't wish that upon anyone.

You may be wondering why I'm telling my story now after staying quiet for all of these years as the story of Gary's death spun out of control. I am not interested in fame. I'm donating a percent of proceeds to The L&M Inc., a nonprofit corporation. The proceeds that I receive from this book will go to people who need it: kids who've been mentally and physically abused. And to help the homeless in the USA. Anyone who wants to be part of this is free to help, so I will have a web page set up for anyone who wants to help.

I want to set the record straight and cut through the BS and fictionalized aspects of my friends' stories that have been out in the public for all this time. There's a lot more to this situation than people realize, so much corruption and misinformation. People have come out of the woodwork, trying to reap their own money and fame off what happened, and it's only fueled the imaginary aspects of this story further.

There's still so many misunderstandings about Ricky and Gary. But I was there when Gary died. I saw it all with my own eyes. It happened so fast. I'm doing this for closure and to issue a warning:

these are all the things I wish I could have told my younger self. If you're a teen who finds yourself going down the wrong path with the wrong people, you can always choose a different path. It's not too late to make a change. For parents, watch your kids! Pay attention to them. Be their parents, not their friends. Don't let them out at all hours of the night, indifferent as they drink and do drugs and get into trouble.

I've wanted to write this book for a long time. My family has been worried about my telling my story out of fear how the story will reflect on them. They cared only about their image. I'm done keeping my mouth shut. I need to get this story out. I'm not getting any younger. I don't want to keep going through life with regret.

It's possible to get through the hard times. I've been through a lot of shit, and I'm still standing. The hell I've been through, I'm hoping it'll help others to hang on as they encounter their own struggles. Maybe my story will help someone. If it does, if it makes an impact on even one person, it'll be worth it.

All these years later, I'm tired of seeing people take this story—my story—and twist it up to their own benefit. So here is my story, the good and the bad—all of it.

Albert Quinones U.S. Army 1986

Gary Lauwers

Ricky Kasso

WHO'S WHO

1. Albert Quinones—wrong place at the wrong time
2. Rich Barton—the quiet kid, Albert's neighbor
3. Ricky Kasso—spun out of control
4. Gary Lauwers—happy and invincible
5. Jimmy Troiano—the perfect storm that destroyed the village of Northport
6. Mark Florimonte—loyal friend of everybody
7. Randy Guthler—the gravedigger
8. William Billy Leason—the boy who doesn't stop his lies
9. Robert Atkinson—Albert's good friend
10. Sara Gatto—sweet girl that knew nothing
11. Karen Novollino—helped catch Jimmy

12. Eric Naiburg—new lawyer looking for his name in fame
13. William Keaton—Suffolk County district attorney (DA)
14. Officer Gene Roemer—friend of the family and lead detective
15. Chief Robert Howard—head of Northport Village Police Department, created lies for the name of fame
16. Lori Walsh—the girl who did the right thing, friends of everyone

CHAPTER 1

LET THE TRUTH BE KNOWN

Northport Park

Northport was seen as this perfect place when I was growing up. It wasn't perfect—far from it—but that's how people saw it. Doctors' and lawyers' families lived there, and the garbage was picked up on time every week, and the houses were pretty and neat, with perfectly manicured lawns, and nothing bad happened there. That's how it was seen, anyway.

It was exclusive. The town, with its 7,500 residents, is located on Long Island's north shore, about an hour's drive outside of Manhattan, if traffic is thin. Long Island is a long, thin overcrowded strip of land, and Northport is right in the middle, halfway between New York Harbor and Montauk Point.

The area now called Northport was first inhabited by Native Americans, the Matinecocks, and it was later known for farming and shipbuilding. Northport came to represent good, clean upper-middle-class living.

A farm was located a few blocks from where I grew up. We used to go buy eggs and milk there, They had cows, chickens, and many other animals. My friend Ken Davenport's parents owned it. It's still there. He took it over after they died.

At Crab Meadow Beach, people would hang out and skinny dip and run wild and have barbecues. We were able to do whatever we wanted, which included typical childhood pranks. We'd take bags of dog shit, set them on fire, and put them in front of someone's door so that when they'd stamp it out, they'd get shit all over their shoes, and we'd laugh and laugh. Or bottle rocket fights where we'd have two teams with six guys on a side; we'd load up cans with bottle rockets, and we'd shoot them back and forth, or we'd just chase after each other down the road with the bottle rockets.

When I was in middle school, during the summer when school was open, my friends and I walked into school with this huge can full of bottle rockets, and we shot them off as we walked down the hallway. We got suspended for about a month for that. I wasn't an angel growing up. I was pretty wild, but I lived, and I learned.

We used to play the game Ghost in the Graveyard on the side of my friend Fred Schneider's house, and if you got touched, you were the ghost, and people would chase after you. I remember climbing up a tree, and Fred was climbing up the tree to touch me.

I kicked him off the tree, and he fell into the bushes. He got so mad, he shook the tree, and I fell too. And then I became a ghost because he touched me. We played that all night.

Fred's family had a big backyard. We rode dirt bikes back there, tearing up the grass, and if it started raining, we played soccer in the mud; we were tracking mud everywhere we went. His parents were not happy.

My family used to live near "the sand pit." It was a giant depression carved into the sand cliffs by the Steers Sand and Gravel Co., which used to mine down there. The sand was turned into cement that was used to build things in New York City. Every morning, we'd wake up and watch people go hang glide off the top of the pit down into the sand below. Eventually, they started building condos where "the pit" was located. They used to have the Fireman's Fair down there, with its amusement park rides and games and food.

People performed live music at the park and played checkers. Northport was like living on the TV show *Fantasy Island*, where everything seemed so breezy and so upbeat. Beautiful boats on the water, people walking their dogs—it was like living in a dream.

While everything seemed happy from the outside, my childhood wasn't a dream. My mother and father split up when I was eleven or twelve years old. The rumor was that it was over my dad's drinking, but who knows? That's just what I've heard. She never spoke badly about my dad. After he left, she didn't speak much about him at all. She always kept quiet, even about the things we should have talked about.

I liked my dad…most of the time. Parents can be a pain, you know? He was aggressive when he spoke; he never hit a woman, and he never hit me either, but he was very strong in his mannerisms. When he made a point, you knew he was right. And that's exactly how it was going to go, and that was that. The family's splitting up was tough for him. It was tough for me too.

He imparted a lot of lessons. I remember he told me, "A real man will work for his money and take care of the family." And when I was about ten years old, he had me delivering these penny savers and newspapers. I had to take the newspapers, roll them up, and stick them in these plastic sleeves. And I had to load them in this sack. I had a pile of these papers and had to bike around my route, and he would follow me in his car to make sure I did it. I would say to him, "Why don't you let me ride in the car next to you? Then I could chuck the newspapers out the window?"

"No," he said, "that's too easy. You gotta go down the hard road before you start taking it easy because if you keep going the easy way, you're never going to know what's on the other side. You might need to help down the road one day."

That applied to riding my bike too. He wanted me going all the way around the block, not cutting through yards.

You never knew what was on the other side of the block. He made me deliver those papers in rain and snow. I felt like a mailman. And he made me carry the umbrella with me as I walked. I wasn't happy, but at the end of the week, it felt good getting a paycheck, even if he ended up taking half of it. "Hey, I had to go with you," he said.

When I was older, he gave me the money back so I could buy a car. It was definitely a learning experience. I won't forget that.

During my teen years, I wanted to stay with my father, but my mother didn't want that. She had so much anger and resentment over him, she didn't even want him seeing us. My father had a huge argument with my mother about it. He wanted to see me and be with me. "You will never see your son again as long as you're alive," she told him.

As a little boy, your father is your hero. He's the man you think you need to grow up to be. Fathers are strong and powerful and smart and fun. And as you get older, you start to recognize how imperfect they are. They're as flawed as the next person; they're just trying their best to make sense of the world and provide for their family and pass on their lessons.

I was never allowed to come to that realization with my dad and fully understand him for the man he was. My mother kept me from building a relationship with him. Maybe she had her reasons for keeping us apart, but she never explained them. And there were points in my life when I definitely needed a father figure, and he wasn't there.

No matter how mad my mother was at him, she didn't deserve to take him away from us. But I didn't just lose my dad; she kept us away from my dad's entire side of the family; aunts, uncles, cousins—all gone from my life. And she drove her own side of the family away too. My mother's mother, my grandmother, lived with us for a while; she lived downstairs. My mother wasn't home at night, so my grandmother was always around. Then all of a sudden, I came home from school, and she was gone—meaning, I had no one.

I took all of that anger and those feelings of neglect and poured that energy and focus into sports, where I could tackle and pin people and make them feel the way that I felt inside. I could feel like I was better than someone else, even for just a few minutes. After the game or match was over, I was back to feeling like shit again. But while the game was going on, I couldn't be stopped.

I saw sports as my ticket out of my situation, something that was going to open up lots of opportunities for me. I was a super-jock. I played football and soccer and wrestled. I was on a travel soccer team, and at fourteen, I had people looking at me and thinking I might go to a major college or the Olympics. In wrestling, I was always competing against bigger opponents. I used to demolish everyone in my weight class.

I had soccer games and wrestling meets, and my mother was never there. After travel soccer finished out in Massapequa, which was thirty miles away and on the South Shore of Long Island, she never showed up, so I had to figure out how to get back, which meant either getting a ride to the train station or asking a fellow soccer player to give me a ride.

My mother paid more attention to my sisters Debbie and Wendy than me (I also have three older half sisters). Debbie is one year older than me, while Wendy is one year younger than me. I was right in the middle.

I was brought up with a very clear sense of manners. When a woman has a problem, you do the right thing and don't expect anything in return. You open a door for a woman. Give them respect and be the protector and a helper. If someone disrespected any of the women in my family, I had to step in and take care of it. If the car broke down, I'd go in there and try to fix it because that was a man's job, and I was the man of the household by default.

On the flip side, having sisters meant I was always dating my sister's friends. I was falling in love and having fun. It cost ninety-nine cents to go to the movies. You could slip a dollar out of your mom's pocketbook and spend the day there.

I get that it's a lot for a single parent to stay on top of their children, but I had zero supervision. My friends and I pretty much did whatever we wished. It was the tail end of the era of peace and love, the late 1970s and early 1980s. Parents didn't care. We used to have wild parties at my house almost every weekend and people would come over and party.

One time, it turned into like 250 people at the house. The whole block was packed with cars and motorcycles. The house didn't get trashed or anything, but there were lots of people to the point where you couldn't even get down the road. It was a wild night. We had lots of wild nights. We were young and dumb. We were invincible.

And even with all the wild times, at least where I was concerned, there was no real discipline involved. I never got grounded or anything. That's just how it was back then growing up in Northport.

I went to school with the same group of kids. We all went to elementary school and middle school and high school together. I was friends with just about everyone, but I got the closest to Gary and Ricky. They were like brothers to me.

CHAPTER 2

WHO WE WERE

GROWING UP, MY friends were my support system. When we had problems with our families, we spoke about them with each other. We always unquestioningly embraced each other and tried to lift each other up. We talked openly and expressed our feelings with zero inhibition. If one of us had a problem in school, we'd calm him down so he didn't do anything stupid.

When everything went down, if it wasn't for my friends, I don't know what would've happened to me. They prevented me from having a breakdown. I had nowhere else to turn. I couldn't speak to my mother or my sisters. They wouldn't let me talk about what happened in the house. With my friends, as well, it was different.

Gary Lauwers was a good kid. When his parents cut him off, though, he got into stealing. They had found out that he was smoking weed and doing other drugs at sixteen or seventeen. Honestly, we were all smoking weed and experimenting because we had no parental supervision. Eventually, Gary got hooked on drugs and robbed everyone.

Gary was a good guy, but he grew out of control and developed a bad reputation. He looked like a little angel—deep-blue eyes, blond hair. He didn't deserve what happened to him. His parents had tried to help him, but it was too late. He was partying, doing drugs, doing whatever he wanted. His parents should've been on top of him. They failed him.

Ricky was always quiet and shy, the opposite of a loudmouth. He never stole a thing. He'd always ask permission before borrowing stuff. He was always the person who sat in the background and kept to himself. He was worried about being ridiculed. He had a tough time at home, and he'd numb himself with drugs to avoid facing his inner demons.

Ricky, Gary, and I grew up together. We lived in the same neighborhood, went to elementary school together, were on the same soccer team, and had the same teachers. We went everywhere together: the park, the beach, and the movies.

Jimmy, on the other hand, didn't grow up in Northport. He was from upstate. Jimmy Troiano was always in and out of juvenile detention and jail, mostly for robbing and stealing. Rumor has it, Jimmy once stole a gun, only to use it in order to carjack someone else's car on his way home from working as a district attorney at the Suffolk County Islip court building and held him at gunpoint and took his car. For Jimmy, he's a criminal to this day. He's currently back in jail serving time for fifteen years for robbing a CVS.

In high school, everything changed. I was out of control. I started selling drugs, primarily weed and cocaine. I had a lot of anger after my parents split up. My mother resented me because I reminded her of my father. Ricky and Gary were still on the same page as I was, dealing and doing drugs. We all went to the same parties and got wild and had fun.

Ricky's stepfather was the coach of the Northport football team in junior high. He was always very pushy. Ricky didn't like him very much. His mother never stood by Ricky's side or defended him, even though the stepfather was an arrogant jerk. She was scared of him. At one point during our drug spiral, Ricky's mother put Ricky in rehab. After he returned, his stepfather beat him up on the football field with his helmet and called him horrible names. When Ricky went home that night, his stepfather kicked him out of the house simply because Ricky didn't want to play football. He moved into my house and became part of our family.

Gary, too, was always over at my house, especially once things got serious between him and my sister Debbie. I didn't know about their romance at first, but when I found out, Gary Lauwers and we didn't talk for a little while. Eventually, I realized I didn't have a right to be upset with Gary or my sister since I dated my sister's friends all the time. Ultimately, their relationship brought all of us closer together.

Gary stole anything that wasn't nailed down and tried to sell it. He'd steal the shoes off one friend and sell them to another friend in the same social group. There was no logic. He never stole from me, though, since he was scared of what I'd do, and he was always at my house. He knew that I'd kick his ass if he ever tried anything with me. We'd go to parties, and he'd take anything valuable—jewelry, money, etc. He developed a reputation, and eventually, no one trusted him.

Gary's kleptomania caused him problems. His parents kicked him out and sent him to rehab many times over. Gary went missing so often that when he went missing on that fateful night, no one thought anything of it.

Gary's father was a plumber who owns his own business and worked in Manhattan, so he made good money. He took care of the house, and the wife stayed home and took care of the kids, but they couldn't keep Gary under control. He must've been having problems with his mother since his last words were, "Tell my mother I love her."

Gary and I were on the same traveling soccer team in junior high and high school. I remember that he played center field and goalie. At one of our games, my older sister Debbie hooked up with him, and they fell in love. This made everything more complicated when everything went to hell. There I was, friends with both Gary and Ricky, and my sister was going out with one of them.

We all used to water ski together, go to fairs together, and go to the movies together. My sister was into sports too. She was on the volleyball team. As time went on, when my friends gained a reputation for their thievery, no one wanted to be around them. I didn't let that keep me from being friends with them. As long as they didn't do wrong by me, it was all good.

Jimmy came into the picture later on when we were in junior high. Before then, he was in some type of boarding school and juvie. He'd been arrested for robbing his neighbors upstate, so his parents wanted to get him out of that area and start a new life. Just before school was released for summer break, he came to Northport.

Jimmy was an arrogant jerk. He had no friends. No one wanted to be around him. He was an instigator. He robbed everything, but he didn't care; he had no remorse. He would pull a gun on you and steal your car. He would break into your house and rob you of everything without thinking twice. He didn't think about anything. He scared a lot of people.

On that fateful night, I believe Jimmy provoked Ricky into fighting Gary. If it weren't for Jimmy, the tragedy would never have happened. Jimmy kept wanting to be a part of my friend group, maybe because I sold drugs. I didn't like him. Every time I told him to get lost, he'd try to connect with a friend of mine instead. He tried this with Ricky too. Jimmy was always kept at arm's length. That fateful night, he was with us because I felt bad. Ricky, Jimmy, and Gary were not allowed at the birthday party I'd been invited to, and I was not about to abandon them.

MEMORIES

The first time Ricky, Gary, and I smoked weed was in the Northport VA hospital area. I was going down there for school, and I saw the two of them in the woods. As I walked by, they called me up to join them. They asked me if I wanted to smoke with them, and I accepted. We were about thirteen years old. We got the munchies, and I invited them over my house to eat a bunch of cookies before my mom got home. We made a complete mess of the kitchen.

One night, the three of us, along with a few others, got really stoned and decided to go to the VA hospital. We broke through the VA hospital fence and climbed up and painted graffiti all over the VA water tower. When we got to the top, our friend Mark pulled out spray paint cans that he'd taken from my garage. We got to work.

The next day, they wanted to go back and go up there to do it again. For some reason, I didn't go up there a second time, maybe because my mother had grounded me for something else. But I could see the water tower from my house. Sirens were going off, and I saw lights flashing on the water tower. My friends climbed almost to the top, but the helicopters were flying over them, and cops surrounded them. Apparently, they had expected us to return after our first night there. The cops yelled at them to come down. They all got arrested. In hindsight, it wasn't very bright to put our names on the tower. They were bailed out quickly by their parents and had to pay for the repainting of the water tower.

The first concert that Ricky, Gary, and I went to was Santana in Manhattan by the pier. We were told that we weren't allowed in the city, but we went anyway. We waited in line for a long time; it took an hour to get our tickets. As we were waiting, people were selling cookies on the side and we had just finished smoking weed, and we had the munchies, as usual. We bought the cookies for fifteen dollars each, but we didn't care about the price.

It turned out that the cookies had LSD in them. There we were in the early evening, inside the concert hall, with the US Navy fleet in the scene's backdrop. The concert included a laser beam show with the battleships behind us. We were tripping out. It looked like the ships were shooting torpedoes behind us. That was our first concert together.

After the concert, we didn't make the train home in time. We ended up sleeping in the park in Manhattan. I couldn't wait for the acid trip to end. Early in the morning, we made it onto the train and returned home to Long Island.

I hung out with the misfits, the people whom no one else liked. People used to pick on our friend Philip because he was so small. I was his protector, a big brother figure. I'd whip anyone's ass who attacked my friends. I was big for my age, which helped. I also had a lot of aggression and anger, as I'd mentioned earlier. I took my anger out on everyone in my line of sight. My wrestling coach would always place me in a higher weight class, and I'd still win.

We used to have parties at my friend Billy's house. His father was a very well-known lawyer, so they had a nice house on the beach at Eatons Neck. One night, Ricky, Gary, our friend Roudy, and I decided to get lobsters and clams from the water, so we took Roudy's father's boat and pinched a bunch of them out of the local harbor. We stuffed them all in black bags, went to Billy's house for a party, and busted out all of the food. We were the hit of the party. That was also the night that Gary stole Ricky's drugs, and it was the beginning of Gary's downfall.

To be precise, Gary stole one hundred tabs of acid and money from Ricky. Ricky was embarrassed that his friend robbed him in his sleep. He never said anything until a few weeks later, when we went to the movies one night. Honestly, that's when everything came to a head. Ricky was trying to save money to get in an apartment because his pride was wounded over staying with us.

One afternoon, Philip Morell, Mike Desterno, and Ricky were hanging out at Ricky's house. Ricky had eaten some acid and had gone into the bathroom. After he had been in there for about ninety minutes, we knocked on the door out of concern. He told us that he was on the phone, but back then, there were no cell phones. Ricky's stepfather kicked the door down and grabbed him by his shirt. He yelled at everyone to get out of his house and began beating Ricky to a pulp. That was Ricky's life in a nutshell—drugs, embarrassment, and a broken home.

It wasn't very surprising that when Ricky got arrested, he was wearing his ACDC concert. That was the era. If you didn't have a rock concert shirt on, you weren't cool. We had all gone to that concert back in 1982 or so. We'd gone to Jones Beach to see Ozzy Osbourne. We tried to sneak down to the first row, but the security guards yelled at us and told us to return to our seats higher up. I told my friends that during intermission, we should take off and sneak down to the front row. We went off in different directions, and they caught some of us, but I managed to get to the front row.

Eventually, it started to rain, and people left, but it didn't bother me. The last song Ozzy played was "Crazy Train." It was badass. He was impressed that I stayed through the rain, so he invited me and ten other people, mostly girls, to go backstage with him. I was ecstatic. I was about to head backstage, but I told Ozzy that I couldn't go because my friends had been kicked out and that I couldn't hang out with him without my friends. I couldn't leave them stranded. Ozzy told me that he respected that and that no one had ever turned this down before. Maybe I was too loyal back then. Maybe I wouldn't have gotten involved in the tragedies to come if I'd looked out for myself over other people.

CHAPTER 3

THE DAY IT HAPPENED

Gary Lauwers

ALBERT QUINONES

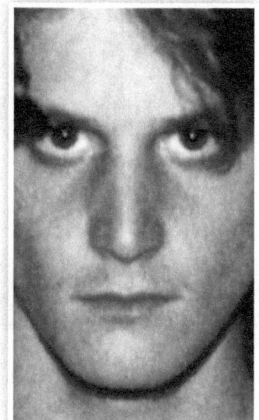

Ricky Kasso

Albert Quinones 1984

EYEWITNESS

The map leading to the crime scene from Northport Park

Gary was part of my family because we grew up together and he was going out with my sister, Debbie Quinones, and Ricky was part of my family because we grew up together. Telling you about what happened between Ricky Kasso and Gary is very painful for me, but you need to hear the truth.

Around noon on June 16, 1984, my mom was nowhere to be found, as usual. Gary had come over to see Debbie and me. Truthfully, he pretended like he wanted to see me, but of course, he really just wanted to spend time with his girlfriend. It wasn't a big deal since we all hung out together anyway. We were like a giant family; my friends were my sister's friends and vice versa.

After hanging at my house, we went to the beach. Everyone from our crew was there with us. We caught wind that Chuck Chesire's girlfriend might be throwing Chuck a surprise birthday party that night.

After the beach, we went back to my house for a delicious barbecue, baby back ribs with a glazed barbecue sauce, hamburgers, hotdogs, and grilled mushrooms and onions. We started drinking, smoking weed, and dabbling in cocaine. Of course, Ricky had weed and acid with him because that was his thing.

Later in the early evening, we headed down to Northport to hang out at the docks. Every weekend, there'd be dance parties at the docks' infamous Gazebo. It was always free, and it was always a good time. Billy Joel performed there once. The girls we were with decided to meet up with us there later in the night, so Ricky, Gary, a few other guys, and I had gone down to Northport without them.

We ate at the docks and smoked more weed. By around six or seven at night, the girls finally came down to meet us. All of Northport High School and junior high was in the area since that was really the only place to hang out at night. It was a fun scene: boats, docks, music, and drinks.

It turned out that Chuck's girlfriend, Sangrine, was having a party after all. Just before we were told about it, Jimmy showed up at the docks. I knew that no one would have wanted Jimmy, Ricky, or Gary at the party, and I didn't blame them; they had terrible reputations! And the rest of the kids didn't experience the kind hearts that I knew Ricky and Gary had. Anyway, we all headed over to her place around nine or ten.

Everyone was there. When we arrived, Sangrine told me that she didn't want Jimmy, Ricky, and Gary at her house, just like I predicted. I told her that I wouldn't leave my friends. Ricky was staying at my place at the time, and there was no way I was going to leave him. Regardless of their reputations, they were loyal to me, and I wanted to be loyal in return.

Until this point, there was no mention of the fact that Gary had stolen Ricky's acid. Hell, no one had said anything the entire week leading up to the night of Sangrine's party. So I figured it was water under the bridge by now. It was one hundred tabs, so it probably only cost Ricky about one hundred dollars anyway.

I jokingly told the guys that I was stuck with them. They wanted us to crash the party even though they weren't welcome, but I insisted that would be wrong and would only lead to trouble. I told them that we'd just have to make the best of it and have a fun night on our own terms. "Maybe we can go into the Aztakea Woods and just hang out and do acid," I said to them.

I'd done acid once or twice before. This night would've been the third time. We figured we'd start a small fire when we got to the woods. There was a big lot in the woods with no trees but nice green grass that extended for a mile. It was beautiful.

EYEWITNESS

It started raining hard enough that the ground was wet. We left Northport and did a tab of acid before we headed to the woods since I figured it would take an hour for the drugs to kick in. As we started walking from Northport Park, we went east on Main Street and made a right on Laurel Avenue gojng south to 25. We went west then made a right on Church Street, going north, then made a left on Franklin Street, and it felt like the longest walk of my life. The acid had kicked in earlier than I'd expected.

The four of us stopped at Dunkin' Donuts around eleven at night. I figured that since I had a friend who worked there, he'd give us any remaining food they had for free. In return, I'd give him weed in a couple of days. As we walked to the 25-A, Jimmy and Ricky lagged behind Gary and me for some reason. That annoyed me since I thought they were being passive-aggressive. The acid didn't help.

Gary thought it was weird too. He asked me, "Is everything all right? Is Ricky still pissed at me?"

"About what?" I replied.

"About the drugs I stole from him."

"I doubt he's mad," I said. "Did you square up with him?"

"Well, you need to take care of it, Gary, okay?"

I shrugged it off, and the four of us got to Dunkin' Donuts. We drank sodas and ate doughnuts for free. We were given so much and were tripping so hard that we threw a bunch of it out. When you're high on acid, you tend not to have much of an appetite.

Eventually, we arrived at the woods. Everyone was very quiet. It was a little awkward since usually we'd always talk even if it was just about stupid shit. Apparently, Ricky had done five more hits of acid on top of the two hits he'd taken earlier.

We wanted to start a fire, but the wood was too wet. Gary said that he'd cut off the sleeves of his jacket to use for the fire instead. He also wanted to fit in with the rest of us since we all wore cutoff sleeves. It worked, and we sat watching our little blaze.

Gary and I were on one side of the fire, and Ricky and Jimmy were on the other side. Ricky and Jimmy were whispering to each other, which I hated. Even to this day, I don't like it when people whisper. If you have something to say, say it so that everyone can hear.

We smoked more weed, and we were definitely tripping on acid by then. Out of nowhere, Ricky said to Gary, "You know, you still owe me money. You disrespected me. That was wrong. I trusted you like a brother, and you robbed me. It's been over a month now, and you haven't even made an effort to pay me back."

Jimmy and I were just standing back. In my mind, and I'm not positive, I thought Jimmy had put a bug in Ricky's ear back when they were whispering to each other. I think Jimmy provoked Ricky. Jimmy was that way, a coldhearted prick who always wanted to poke the hornet's nest.

Under all of those drugs, Jimmy managed to influence Ricky. Don't get me wrong. What Ricky did was wrong, and I was furious with him afterward, but he wasn't the kind of kid who would murder. I'm not justifying what he did but merely explaining.

Ricky and Gary agreed to have a fight to erase the debt Gary owed. They started fighting. At first, Gary was winning. Jimmy ran over and kicked Gary, which caused Gary to fall off Ricky as I pushed and yelled at Jimmy, then Ricky gained the upper hand. Jimmy and I continued to watch and let them deal with their issue like men. Eventually, Ricky had Gary around the neck. Then Ricky grabbed a knife from his pocket and stabbed Gary one time in the back.

"What the hell are you doing?" I yelled. "Are you kidding me, bro? You're doing this over some stupid bullshit?"

"Stay the hell away from me!" Ricky yelled back. "He disrespected me!"

"Give me the knife!"

He swung the knife at me. Jimmy and I still stood back. I don't know what Ricky was thinking. He swung again at me, and he was not letting go of the knife. "What he did was wrong, and he's gonna go to hell for it," Ricky said to me.

When I tried to take the knife away from Ricky again, Gary broke free from Ricky, and as he tried to run past, Jimmy then stuck his leg out and tripped Gary. Ricky then grabbed Gary around the neck again, but I failed to stop Ricky.

"Tell my mother I love her," he said to me. "Tell my mother I love her," Gary shouted.

And then Ricky stabbed him in the back and chest. He stabbed him so many times, I lost count—eyes, neck, and chest. He stabbed Gary in the neck, hitting the jugular vein, and the blood sprayed all over my face. And I was covered in blood. Ricky wouldn't stop.

I was in shock. I didn't know what to do or what to say. I was sick to my stomach. *This is not happening*, I thought.

Gary's body was lying on the ground, clearly not breathing. No one said anything. At this point, Jimmy and I didn't want to go near Ricky since he was out of his mind, standing there with his knife in his hand then just a while ago. The body was lying on the ground and had muscle convulsions. Ricky hopped on the body and started stabbing it repeatedly over and over again till the body was lying back down. He was stabbing Gary in his face and his chest too many times to count with a knife that Jimmy gave Ricky from stealing from the Midway.

Eventually, I spoke. "You just killed our friend!"

"Dead men can't speak!" Jimmy said merrily. "You better not say anything," he said to me. "Or you're next." Jimmy then said to Ricky, "Let's move the body from the camp fire."

Ricky grabbed Gary's arms, and Jimmy grabbed Gary's legs. Then they dragged him into the woods as I stood by the campfire in shock.

"Are you kidding me, you asshole?" I snapped.

I was covered in blood from when Ricky was stabbing Gary in the jugular vein of his neck. It sprayed all over my face, and I could not see anything. I just wanted out of the woods. I knew if I didn't play cool, I was going to be the next one laying down next to Gary because they had nowhere else to go to clean up and change their clothes. I think that was why they let me live. I said, "Let's go to my house, change our clothes, and clean ourselves before my mother gets home." I knew they had nowhere else to go. That's why they let me live.

We didn't bother to check Gary's pulse. Maybe the drugs scared us too much, or maybe there was just so much blood that it was obvious he was dead.

The three of us started walking back to my house. We were quiet the entire way. "We're all going to go to jail over some stupid shit!" I hissed when we arrived at my house. "We're gonna change our clothes, and then you both gotta go."

That was the first and last time that Jimmy came to my house. He was never my friend, and now I knew it. To this day, I hate him.

Recently, I saw an interview with Jimmy. The interviewer asked if he was angry about what happened. He said that he hoped Ricky said his prayers before he hung himself up with no remorse. He was never really a friend of any of us. I think that Jimmy convinced Ricky that no one would respect him, that everyone would have thought he was a wimp if he had done nothing about Gary's theft.

We bagged all of our clothes, showered, put on new clothes, and then I told them to take their bags of clothes and leave. And they left.

THE FOLLOWING DAYS

The next day, I felt like I was in a dream. I was still shocked and even nauseated at last night's tragedy. I remember not tasting food. I was in shock, not knowing which way to turn, not being able to talk to anyone, walking around in a daze, trying to process what really happened I was having a hard time. Not knowing how to process the murder, my mind retreated into numbness and emptiness.

The following evening around five, I went down to Northport Village with a few friends. There, I saw Ricky and Jimmy. Ricky was really upset. He looked flustered and white, and he couldn't believe what he had done. I rehashed what he did back to him, and he started crying and apologizing. He still had the knife on him. I told him to get rid of it, so he threw it into Northport Harbor by the Gazebo.

Northport Harbor—Where Ricky Kasso threw the knife/murder weapon into the harbor

EYEWITNESS

We all went our own separate ways after that. I was pretty disgusted with Jimmy and Ricky, so I just hung out with my other friends. I have no idea where the two of them went.

The next day, I found out that Jimmy had taken a gun, stood in the middle of Middleville Road, and carjacked a lawyer's car. He and Ricky used it to go upstate to Saratoga. They were gone for a couple of days. When I heard, I couldn't believe it. I was worried that they'd rat me out. Now that I'd distanced myself from Ricky, I figured that if they got caught, they'd pin the murder on me. I told a couple of friends about what Ricky did to Gary but did not give them details of why, how, and when it happened because I needed to talk to someone. When Mark and Richie Barton told me that Jimmy had taken them to see the body, I did not respond to it. I left it alone. I just told Rich and Mark that Ricky and Jimmy went upstate. We were at my house, smoking weed like always. Then a police officer knocked on my door. I recognized him from the streets. We used to call him and his partner Tweedledee and Tweedledum. He told me that he received a call that someone was robbing a house and wanted me to go with him as his backup. I knew it was bullshit and said, "Not a problem. I'll go with you."

Maybe my friends didn't try to stop me because they didn't think the police knew anything yet, and we were high from smoking weed. I had a bad feeling it was going down now. I got in the car with the cop, and we drove down the road. The next thing I knew, there were three undercover cops driving in front, alongside, and behind our car. They grabbed me out of the car and put me in one of the unmarked cars. I sat in the middle of the backseat, surrounded by cops. I was so scared, so nervous. They started asking me questions. "Where's Gary?"

"I don't know."

"We know you know."

They took me to the courthouse off Motor Parkway in Smithtown and kept me there until late at night. I wasn't even given a chance to make a call. I found myself sitting in what I gathered was an interrogation room. They kept asking about Gary, Ricky, and Jimmy, but I refused to give them anything.

"We know you were there that night."

"I don't know anything."

They started hitting me. They kept me there for over four hours, beating me for much of the time, but I didn't say a word. They threw me against the wall. They made me spread my arms and legs against the walls and then kicked me in the genitals and punched me in the ribs many times. They even hit me in the head so many times that I was having double vision and headaches for a week.

I agreed to a polygraph test, so they put probes all over my body and asked me more questions. But you have to be calm for a polygraph test, and I was so nervous that they couldn't get an accurate reading.

They decided to let me go. They drove me back in the undercover car, and the detective gave me his phone number. "If you hear anything, give us a call," the detective said.

"After four and a half hours of beating me, I doubt I'll be calling you."

I went back into my house at 3:30 a.m. Everyone was still there, wondering where I had been, so I told them that I went for a walk. Privately, I told Rich and Mark Florimonte the truth. At first, they didn't believe me. I lifted my shirt up, and they saw all of the bruises on my stomach and ribs. They were in shock. "Oh shit, it's going down," Rich said.

Another day went by. From what I've been told, before Ricky and Jimmy went upstate, Jimmy spoke with Karen Novellion Laurie and Walsh and told her that Ricky killed Gary. Then she told her father. Her father was a police officer from Northport, but I don't think Jimmy knew Laurie Walsh's father was a police officer from Northport and that Laurie told her father everything, and that's how the word got out about Gary's murder.

The police went into Northport Aztakea Woods and found the body covered in leaves. The night Gary was murdered, Ricky and Jimmy had carried Gary's body to a spot where they could not hide Gary's body well enough. I stayed by the campfire. I was worried that if I'd ran, Ricky might've killed me too.

I was surprised that it took so many weeks for the police to find Gary's body. To me, every passing day felt like a month. That's when the shit really hit the fan. I had a feeling that they'd come back to my house, so I called a few friends who knew already and suggested that we just take off to the docks. That way, they wouldn't humiliate me in front of my family. We went down to Northport Docks with a bucket and fishing poles. We started fishing, just waiting for the cops to get me.

We heard the police sirens, and a whole gang of cop cars came to the docks. They drove right onto them to block them off. There must've been fifty of them as well as helicopters and dogs. They drove all the way to the end of the docks. They grabbed all of us, separated us, and brought us to the Northport Village police department. We were all placed in separate rooms.

They kept asking me questions about Gary and Ricky, and I kept pleading ignorance. "We know what happened. We got Ricky and Jimmy in the other room. They told us that you had nothing to do with it."

I hadn't realized that they'd come back from upstate. "I don't know what's going on."

"We know what happened, Albert. Just tell us the truth. Ricky already told us that he killed Gary, that he's taking responsibility."

I still denied it, and then the cop brought Ricky into the room. "Albert, I told them I did it," Ricky said. "I'm sorry about what happened. Tell your mom

I'm sorry. I didn't mean for this to happen. Please, just tell them the truth."

They took Ricky away, and I made a statement. I told them what happened, but the detectives didn't want to hear the story that I told them. They wanted me to nail Jimmy too.

They told me to say that Jimmy held Gary down, gave Ricky the knife, and helped him kill Gary. I told them that that wasn't what happened. "We don't care. Jimmy's a dirt bag, and we want to lock his ass up. We will only give you immunity if you tell us that Jimmy played a part in Gary's murder."

I suspected that the DA was behind this. I signed the papers that I'd testify in court and say what they wanted to hear, and only then did they bring me home. Police officer Jean Romeo folded my mother what happened, and she was in shock. The DA told my mother that if I stood by my statement, I'd be fine. I'd confess to the two of them having murdered Gary.

By then, reporters were all over the place. News anchors were outside the police station. The chief of police had made a statement that a cult of devil worshippers murdered Gary. The media went wild with this. Even though the police later retracted their statements, it was too late.

Reporters camped outside my house too, asking for statements from me, but I wouldn't speak to them. I didn't even speak to my mother or sister about what happened. By this time, I didn't talk to my friends about the chaos, either because I was worried that I'd get them into trouble.

Everywhere I went, there reporters were. They made me paranoid. One day, I went to my friend Rich's house, and *Rolling Stone* reporters were in the house. They wanted to speak with me. I started to, but then my mother walked in. She took me out of the house and then yelled at Rich's mom. So the complete interview never happened.

I tried to figure out whether or not the detectives were setting me up. After all, they wanted me to lie in court in order to receive immunity. I was so paranoid. If I was caught lying in court, I'd go to jail for perjury. And if I didn't lie, would they lock me up for being an *accomplice* to a murder?

I was also worried that my house was bugged. With nowhere safe to go, I went to church and talked to the priest during confession, but I stopped myself and walked out on him. I figured he knew it was me.

The DA kept bringing me back to his office for four-hour sessions every day for weeks. They were coaching me on what to say in court. I kept making mistakes because I'm not a good liar. It felt like they were brainwashing me.

Meanwhile, Ricky had hung himself in jail. I didn't understand how he could get away with that since he was on suicide watch with cameras everywhere. Apparently, he used the bedsheets to hang himself. A lot of people say that the police actually killed him.

As weeks went on and everything continued to be publicized, I was placed even further under the microscope. The DA and my mother encouraged me to flee to Georgia for a month or two; things were getting too hot. It was too much commotion. I stayed with my mother's friends, with whom I used to go to church. It was the DA who had suggested I leave since he saw how stressed I was. Needless to say, any chance of my earning a scholarship was gone.

When I finally went to testify, I refused to lie. I told the judge exactly what happened the night that

Gary died. I took the chance that they'd lock me up. The DA and his people were pissed at me, but I did not want to see Jimmy go to jail for something he didn't do. I remember the DA's face when I told the truth—he was in shock.

This made the papers all over again. The press said that I lied. I couldn't get a break! I just wanted to do the right thing. Because I told the truth in court, their attempts to trip me up all failed.

The trial never should've gone on for as long as it did. Jimmy's lawyer was a man named Eric Naiburg. He was just starting his practice at the time. This trial was a huge opportunity for him. Jimmy's defense lawyer didn't have a case to work with since I told the truth, but he wanted to make a circus out of it. Within the first five minutes of my statement, it all should've been over. I told them that Jimmy did not hold Gary down, did not stab him. With Ricky's hanging, that should've been the end of it, but they wanted an eye for an eye.

They continued to examine me for weeks. Eric kept asking me the same question in different ways, trying to trip me up. I think that he wanted to catch me in a lie so that I would be discredited. I eventually told him to move on, and the entire jury laughed at him.

Looking back, I wonder if the DA and Jimmy's lawyer were colluding together from the very beginning. The trial was a big break for Eric, and the DA wanted us to be punished. I think they were hoping that Jimmy would be locked up following my testimony and that I'd be imprisoned for perjury.

Someone had to go down, but I screwed up the DA's plan, and I did the right thing. As much as I hate Jimmy to this day, I couldn't put him behind bars for a murder that he didn't commit.

CHAPTER

ROLLING STONES

ON NOVEMBER 22, 1984, *Rolling Stone* published an article about Gary's murder and "the lost kids of Northport." From the very title, it was wrong: "Cult Killing: Kids in the Dark." We were never in a cult.

The article opens with the graphic discovery of Gary's body. A police dog discovered a "pile of bones wearing a denim vest, running pants, white undershorts, Nikes." The author of the article, David Breskin, described the poor state of Gary's mangled body after worms had gotten to him. According to the article, between fifteen and thirty teenagers had heard about the murder but kept their mouths shut until one girl called the police anonymously to tip them off.

The lies really begin in the fourth paragraph. The author writes that Ricky "Kasso had been charged in April with digging up a grave the previous fall. (Gary Lauwers was among those who watched.)" This never happened.

Then the article spreads the falsehood that Gary was a member of a satanic cult. Breskin appeals to the words of Suffolk County investigators. According to those investigators, numerous chanting cult members witnessed the sacrificial slaughter of Gary. The article gets a little confusing since it admits that Gary was "not particularly close" to the actual satanic cult that had been selling drugs and burning cats in the area. But the article also says that Gary "did those things well enough on his own." More lies.

In a *Washington Post* article, also published in 1984, Margot Hornblower spread similar falsehoods. The second paragraph reads,

> The playground at the foot of Main Street was a gathering place for Richard Kassa, 16, and his

devil-worshipping friends who formed a cult they called The Knights of the Black Circle.

Hornblower went on to accuse us of spray-painting symbols of the Antichrist, a pentagram, and a star that represents the devil on the playground's jungle gym. She connected these lies to the fact that we loved Black Sabbath and Ozzy Osbourne, which was true! But that certainly didn't make us cult members.

The *Washington Post* article referred to police reports, just like the *Rolling Stone* article did. Hornblower wrote that "police said that Kassa confessed to stabbing Lauwers repeatedly, forcing him to say 'I love Satan,' and later gouging out his eyes." A few paragraphs later, she added,

> Suffolk County police and prosecutors say the loose satanic cult of which Kasso was a member is at least three years old… More than 20 [teenagers] are thought to have participated in its rituals, while using mescaline, LSD,

"angel dust," and other drugs that were freely available in the playground in the evening.

And again, Hornblower tied our supposed satanic rituals to our love for rock albums and music videos.

It's true that when Ricky was arrested, he was wearing an AC/DC shirt with a picture of the devil on it. So what? That was a sign of the times. Nothing more.

In another more recent article, Todd McGovern aped the same slanders about all of us. He wrote that Ricky performed satanic rituals in the woods. His argument was, "Don't believe me? Go ahead and Google his name and that same image will be staring back at you from your computer screen." McGovern later called Jimmy and me "reprobate cohorts." He then lied further and said that the three of us *lured* Gary into the woods. He tore into Ricky's name with no reserve:

> Like any good sociopath, he not only brags about the killing to kids at school, but also describes

> it as a human sacrifice and that Satan had commanded him to kill. When met with [disbelief], Kasso went so far as to take doubters into the woods to view Lauwer's decomposing body.

Ricky never did such a thing.

Jimmy has always been selfish, but he really outdid himself in the years following Gary's murder. To boost his own name and to make a buck, he spread all sorts of lies about what happened. He's leaned into the early media reports about the nonsensical devil worshipping. In a 2008 interview, as part of a documentary called *Satan in the Suburbs*, he had the gall to slander Ricky: "And I definitely was a Christian, so his Satanism was, to me, like a little…it was just him, I guess." This is a lie. Ricky was no more a Satanist than the rest of us. That is to say, not at all. And Jimmy took the opportunity to try to signal to the audience that he was a good, religious kid.

The interviewer asked Jimmy if Ricky seemed crazy when they first met. After telling the interviewer how much Ricky hated football, Jimmy said,

"He got busted for digging an Indian grave for a skull or something. After that, Ricky went to county jail for one or two days."

Jimmy is slick, I'll give him that much. He told that interviewer that he "should've known better. I'm always a believer that bygones will be bygones. Shit happens, and I was just dealt a lucky hand and got out of that mess." He was trying to pose as an innocent bystander who managed to get away from all of the chaos. In reality, he's always been guilty of manipulating Ricky and of lying about everything in the years since Ricky killed Gary.

The interviewer then asked Jimmy how he felt about Ricky after the incident. Jimmy answered,

> I wasn't really pissed at him. I was more pissed at the whole incident, that I was high the night of the murder. I just wished that never happened. Unless something deep in Ricky's mind was, you know, Satanism was really in his head and he had to kill him. I don't know. I was more mad when

> [Ricky] started telling everyone, because I really wanted to forget about it. Even the night we saw Gary, I thought he was letting bygones be bygones. Because it's not like we dragged Gary into the woods; he came to hang out with us. It's just the element of the drugs kicked in.

Ricky wasn't the one who told people about what happened; Jimmy was. He bragged to everyone about what happened. He even offered to show his girlfriend, Karen Novelino, and Lori Walsh, the body.

Toward the end of the interview, the interviewer asked Jimmy if he'd like to say anything to any of the people who were connected to the incident. "I'd like to say hi to Albert," he began. "I haven't seen him. And sorry because he got sent to Georgia because when I was in prison, one of the kids that knew about the murder hit him with a beer bottle. And I guess Albert's parents thought that he was gonna be the next one to get killed." Albert wasn't lying that I was sent to Georgia. But again, he was trying to pose as the good guy.

The lies of our being devil worshippers and cult leaders never stopped. In reality, we were little kids, going with the flow. We innocently listened to Ozzy Osborne and similar bands. To this day, my friends from childhood still wear Rush hoodies. And all of us blame Jimmy Troiano for everything that happened. He was a rotten soul.

Now, Jimmy has been going around, saying that I, too, robbed a graveyard. To this day, people think that we are cult members. The truth is so far from that. My friend Randy is the one who robbed a graveyard before Gary's murder, almost a year prior to the incident. He was with someone else who was totally outside my circle. He said so in a documentary too. Jimmy was in jail and rehab before Gary died. He wasn't even around the year leading up to Gary's death, so he wouldn't have known what kids were up to at the time.

Here's what actually happened: a couple of kids went up to the graveyard and dug up a grave. At the time, I didn't know if they stole anything or not. Randy and Gordon had dug up the grave six months before Gary was killed. It hit the papers, and the Northport chief of police assumed that a grave-digging, devil-worshipping cult did it. He couldn't even get that right since Randy and Gordon were just wild teenagers, not cult members.

Lori Walsh told the authorities that Randy's friend Marcus stole a skull out of the grave. It was eventually found under a mailbox. The cops went to Randy for interrogation. They were on drugs, and they were arrested. Randy had to do community service for his graveyard digging. Then, four or five months after Gary was killed, the chief of police made a statement that Jimmy, Ricky, and I were part of that same cult and that Gary's murder was a satanic ritual. Later, he realized that we weren't, but it was too late for him to retract his statement. The media ran wild with it, and they wouldn't let it go.

Throwing more confusion into the timeline, there was another incident during which people kicked over the stones at a different graveyard. Obviously, there was a lot of mischief in my hometown. And you know what? I wasn't always a great kid, but my close friends and I never dug up a grave.

Since Ricky had hung himself and Jimmy didn't care about anything, I was left alone in this ocean of lies. And to this day, Jimmy is making money off of them. He gets percentages of the interviews that he gives. He tells everyone that we were grave-digging devil worshippers. He's trying to turn Gary's murder into a media circus and make me look like a moron just to make money.

Out of respect to my mother and sisters, I stayed quiet as a kid. And so the lies spread like wildfire—until now.

Sources

David Breskin, "Cult Killing: Kids in the Dark," *Rolling Stone*, November 18, 2019, https://www.rollingstone.com/culture/culture-features/long-island-devil-cult-murder-Ricky-kasso-david-breskin-901069/.

Margot Hornblower, "Youths' Deaths Tied to Satanic Rite," *The Washington Post*, July 9, 1984, https://www.washingtonpost.com/archive/politics/1984/07/09/youths-deaths-tied-to-satanic-rite/3286f188-2636-4dbf-a6eb-9b767f1adb5c/.

EYEWITNESS

SatanInTheSuburbs, "Satan in the Suburbs: Interview with Jimmy Troiano," June 17, 2008, https://www.youtube.com/watch?v=uHjK8rJ83cw.

CHAPTER 5

SARAH—RICKY KASSO'S GIRLFRIEND

I RECENTLY VISITED Ricky's old girlfriend Sara Gatto. She still lives in Northport with two beautiful children and a loving husband. As I approached her door, I was surprisingly emotional. I hadn't seen her in decades, and so many dark memories came rushing back. At the same time, I was happy to be back in Northport. Part of me felt optimistic. Sara and I had a special bond. In fact, I think Jimmy had always been jealous of our bond.

Her husband, Samuel, answered the door and immediately recognized me despite all of the years apart. I had met him in the past, both at their wedding and some other social occasions. "Albert!" he said with a joyous grin. "I didn't know you were in town."

"Hey, Samuel," I uttered, a little nervous. "I was hoping I could talk to Sara about what happened."

He frowned at that. "Um, sure, of course. May I ask why?"

I nodded solemnly. "I'm writing a book. I want to clear the record. You know how out of control the lies got between Jimmy and the media."

Samuel opened her door wider. "Yes, of course. Please, come in. Why don't you sit in our living room and wait for Sara? She's in the shower right now."

"Sure," I replied and took a seat in their living room. It had exactly the feel I figured it would: cozy and lovely, just like Sara had always been.

After ten minutes, Sara walked into the living room, smiling widely at me and dressed in an elegant gown. She handed me a cup of coffee. "Albert, it's lovely to see you. Samuel told me you're writing a book." She took a seat across from me. "Where should we start?" she asked quietly.

I smiled back at her. She always had such a warm heart. It immediately felt like we were back in high school, as if no time had passed. "Thanks, Sara. It's wonderful to see you. Could you tell me what first comes to mind when you think of Jimmy and Ricky?"

"Jimmy has always been this evil human being," she told me. "If it wasn't for him, everything would've been very different in Northwood. I was very young when I met Ricky. I was in seventh grade, and he was a little older than me. He was the kind of kid who didn't have anyone taking care of him. He'd been discarded by his family and the school district. He was a nice guy who had nobody looking out for him. We all lived in the same neighborhood. We were like a family, so we took it upon ourselves, as kids, to look out for each other."

I nodded. "That's how I remember them too. Did you ever see Gary's body? And when did you hear about his murder?"

She took a sip of her coffee. "I didn't know about the murder until the discovery of Gary's body reached the news.

"Jimmy took a lot of people up to the forest to show them Gary's body. He later told me that he had told everyone else to never tell me about the body, so

I didn't know. Other people did, but I had no idea. Jimmy wrote me a letter telling me that Ricky told people not to say anything around me or to me at all about it."

My jaw dropped. "I had no idea he wrote you a letter. I wonder why he did that. Did he actually care about you, or was it some kind of control thing?"

Sara shrugged. "Your guess is as good as mine. I was so young at the time."

"How was your relationship with Ricky between the murder and everything blowing up?"

"I remember going to a party around that time," she said, reminiscing. "Ricky tried to talk to me, but I didn't talk to him because I was mad he had left town without telling me. The next day, the incident was in the paper."

"You were thirteen at the time, right?"

"Yeah, that's right."

I took a big gulp of my own coffee. "Do you remember how you felt after everyone learned what happened? Were you close with Gary?"

"After everything was out in the public, I felt horrible. It was insane that Gary was dead. Gary had been a good friend of mine. He'd dated my friends.

I had spent a lot of time with him. Everything was surreal. My friends and I were so young that our parents barely let us out of the house after the incident. I wasn't even allowed to attend Gary's funeral. I was on lockdown."

"How was your relationship with Ricky after you learned what he did? What happened there?"

"At my young age, I had such empathy for Ricky. I knew he wasn't a horrible person. I knew what psychedelic drugs did to people, and I knew the kind of person Jimmy was, even though I had never interacted with Jimmy before the incident.

"Our first time talking was after he wrote me that letter. I stayed away from him, even when he was with Ricky. He'd beat people up in the park for no reason. He'd want Ricky to beat people up too. That never happened before Jimmy came to town. He was just a very bad influence. Unfortunately, when he came to town from wherever he was before, it really changed the whole dynamic. He was terribly violent, and he brought a lot of drugs into town.

"After everyone found out about the incident, there weren't a lot of people who were friends with both Ricky and Jimmy. People had to make a choice."

I sensed that Sara didn't want to talk much about her relationship with Ricky after the murder, so I didn't press it. Instead, I asked, "How would you describe Ricky?"

"Ricky was never violent or mean. I wouldn't have been friends with him if he ever showed signs of that. He was a goofy lost soul. He didn't have an outgoing personality, no confidence. He was just a discarded human. A lot of people back then had a lot of bravado. Not Ricky."

I nodded, my eyes tearing up. "Yeah, I get that."

"Ricky's mother really tried to get him help, but his stepfather couldn't come to terms with the fact that Ricky was never going to be a giant football player. Ricky never lived up to his expectations."

"A lot of people liked Ricky," I added, "but they didn't like being around him when he was with Jimmy."

Sara nodded. "Jimmy was volatile. You just didn't know what was going to happen."

"I remember how we used to take care of each other," I said. "We took others under our wing. Ricky was like a big brother to you, right?"

"That's right. Even though we dated, he was so much more to me than a childhood boyfriend. Even when I was very young and Ricky and his friends were in middle school, it was all peace, love, and rock 'n' roll. There was never an issue between any of us."

"I remember those times," I said quietly, "and I remember how everything changed after the murder—our social circles even."

Sara nodded. "After news got out about Gary's murder, people changed who they hung out with. No one could be honest about things because you'd be judged. I talk to my children about it all the time. My son is a runner, and he runs past the area where Gary was killed. A friend of his told him about it, so I told my son the truth—that Ricky was a castaway, an abused child. I never went near the drugs that Ricky took, but I know that they made Ricky crazy, and those came from Jimmy."

"Jimmy had no heart," I seethed. "And look at Jimmy now. He's in jail because he held a CVS pharmacy at gunpoint, demanding pills. The judge put him in jail for fifteen years."

Sara blinked in surprise. "Wow, I actually didn't know that. The last time I saw him, he was riding a bicycle with bandages wrapped around him. It was very strange."

"I believe it. So I know you were in middle school when news of Gary's murder broke out. How was your life immediately after that?"

"I went to a different school for my last year of middle school. A lot of people I wasn't friends with just kept talking about the incident, so I needed a fresh start. My mom was a young mom, so she wasn't as worried about me once I got to high school. By then, I hung out with people more my own age."

"I see," I said sadly. "I'm so sorry, Sara."

She smiled at me. "Don't worry, Albert. Everything dissipated at that time, maybe for a reason. You were scooped away to safety, and Ricky had hung himself. I had a counselor during high school, so I had someone I could speak to. That was very helpful."

"It's nice to see you doing will, Sara," I said. "I saw a picture of you and your kids when I walked in. They look happy and healthy. Crazy how little our parents were involved back when we were their age, right?"

Sara nodded passionately. "It was a different time then. Now, everyone is a helicopter parent. Back then, we were completely on our own. You had a great mom, and your sisters were great. Most parents were completely unaware of what was happening. Now, I'm completely upfront with my kids. I try to teach my kids that you don't realize how one moment can change your life. Because of that situation, there was no way that you knew what was going to happen. Having to live through something like that and having it in your brain forever is horrendous. It was a terrible, terrible time.

"I never drink in front of my kids. It's the least I can do to encourage them not to go wild. We used to come home wasted as kids. And look where it led. You know, Albert, any time I'm having a hard time or I'm having an issue with my kids, I think of you as an example of someone who got through the worst thing imaginable. If you get be strong enough to muster through what happened, then I can get through anything."

"Yeah," I said, my eyes down at nearly empty cup of coffee. "That's why I'm writing this book, actually—to help people get through their hard times."

"Albert," Sara said in a motherly tone.

I looked up at her warm eyes.

"I hope you're not beating yourself up over what happened. It wasn't your fault. If anything, it was Jimmy's. You just happened to be there."

A tear slid down my cheek. "Thanks, Sara. I know it wasn't my fault. I still… I just wish I could've stopped it."

There you have it. Ricky's girlfriend agrees that it's all Jimmy's fault—not only Gary's murder but Ricky's downfall too.

William "Bill" Leason

WILLIAM LEASON
(FIRST INTERVIEW)

BILLY LEASON WAS very good friends with Gary when we were growing up, but he was jealous that Gary would always come over my house. Out of his jealousy, he started a lot of rumors around town after Gary's murder. He's always been an arrogant drunk, and he's always shot his mouth off without thinking. And as you'll see, he's the same way now. He helped to spread the rumors that we were cult members. He's been a media whore, running his mouth and lying just to get attention.

I texted him, hoping that we could get on the phone and clear the air. We spoke at nearly midnight and, well, he's the same guy he was when we were kids.

Bill has been working for the same mining company for twenty-six years somewhere out in Texas. These days, he works in the import department as a clerk. He has two stepkids who are twenty-five and twenty-six, whom he met when they were only one and two. I'm happy that things worked out for him. But it doesn't change what he did.

"Billy, how are you doing, brother?" I said at the start of our call.

"I don't know if I'd call you 'brother,' but we have known each other forty-plus years."

"A long time, man. A long time." I was trying to keep the peace so early in our conversation.

"Honest to God," he mumbled, "I probably would've killed you if I saw you twenty years ago."

"Really?"

"Yeah, really," Bill said between chuckles. "I only laugh because the first time we met, we had a fight because of Gary. You were beating on Gary on that hill by the church. I called you out and said,

'You want to beat up on someone? Beat on someone your own size.' And then we fought, which I loved. It was fun."

I smiled at the memory. "Back then, everybody fought for fun. I fought with Joey and Frank all the time too. That's what we did."

"Albert, I enjoyed fighting with you. We fought downtown at parties. I try to explain to people. We would play quarters against each other, and then we we'd get wasted, and we'd beat the snot out of each other."

"I remember, bro," I said. "That's what we did as kids. We got drunk. We fought. We made up. We hugged. We kissed."

"Exactly. That's what we did. I want to say that I forgive you for everything because I know that harboring hate is not good for any soul. I think that if I was there, one of us would've probably died because of what happened."

"It had nothing to do with me, bro," I said defensively. "Sometimes things happen, and it's out of your hands, and you have no control over it. It's like a car accident. You drink, you drive, you hit somebody, they die—that's your fault. But I wasn't the one 'behind the wheel.' I never wanted to see anyone get hurt. That wasn't my thing."

"I believe you, but I know you hated Gary. You beat him up every time you saw him."

"No, I didn't," I said, trying to keep my temper at bay. "Gary and I had our problems, but we were friends. We played soccer together. This is what happens when you're kids. You think I ever wanted to see anyone die? No! No one wanted to see that."

"You liked to beat people up."

"How many people did you beat up?" I asked. "A lot of people! What about Frank? He beat people up too. We all did it. Look, I wanted to call you because I don't like the tension in the air. I never had a problem with you. We all hung out, went to parties together."

"That's what I liked about you. We hung out, we partied, and then we just tried to beat each other up. That was cool with me. Honest to God, Ricky and I beat each other up four or five times. Ricky and I fought with the cops once."

"We did the same thing once too, but we were all good friends, man. Unexpected things happened. We're not like the kids nowadays who are pulling guns out and shooting each other. Remember that big lobster party?"

"Oh, yeah. I woke up behind a school the next morning. A custodian woke me up. My mom went looking for me that night. All I can say is that we were all really messed-up people back then."

"We did our things, you know. In the end, no one wants to see tragedy to anybody. It's sad what happened. If I could do something, I would. But I know you were close with Gary."

"I went to his mom's house for ten years after it happened," Billy replied. "Every time I went there, we talked, laughed, and cried. After ten years, she told me to never come back again because she couldn't handle it. She used to tell me, 'Billy, you protect my son.' And I didn't do it.

"The night that it happened, I went looking for you all everywhere. I was supposed to meet Gary downtown that night, but I couldn't because my parents wanted to take me out to eat. The minute we got out there, I ditched my parents and went downtown. I tried to track you down, but I couldn't. I figured if I found you, maybe I would've died. I really wasn't worried about you, but Jimmy was a scary guy."

"He was a bad egg. He talks all this smack, saying he had no idea and that he had just moved to Northport. I thought you went to Chuck's party along with everyone else that night."

"No, actually the day Ricky and Jimmy got arrested, about an hour before that, Gary's mom called me and asked me if I'd seen Gary. I told her no but that I had been looking for him. Then I called a couple other people, and they said that they were downtown. I found out that they were behind the Midway. I grabbed my dad's gun and went down there. My mom was screaming at me."

"How'd you find out about it?"

"I found out through Daddy. She told me that Ricky killed Gary and that they'd been showing people his dead body. Then Chrissie was freaking out, so I showed up downtown. But there were two cop cars there, so I walked away."

"How long after that did Ricky and Jimmy get caught?"

"That was the same day. If I had to guess, you all killed Gary around June 26. I'm sorry to say, 'You all,' but I know you were there—"

"Just because I was there doesn't mean I'm guilty," I snapped. "Do I feel bad? Yeah. Did I have the knife? No."

"You could've stopped it, man," Billy drawled.

"Who says I could've stopped it? You can't make a statement like that unless you were there and saw what happened. You can't judge someone like that. It's wrong."

"Look, if we're going to continue, uh… I thought I was going to stop drinking, but today is my birthday."

"Oh, I had no idea. Happy birthday, man."

"You're the last person I thought I'd be talking to on my birthday," Billy said. "You ever see *The Walking Dead*? You're Negan."

"Ha! My mother and I used to watch it all the time at her place in Manhattan. Listen, enjoy your birthday-"

"No, no. I got out of bed to talk to you."

"Okay," I said. "How long after Gary's murder did Ricky and Jimmy get caught? I still don't know since I left town right after it happened."

"Here. You tell me what you don't know, and I'll tell you what I know. Maybe we'll come to a place where… I don't hate you as much."

"I wanted to clear the air with you too because I don't want this tension between us. I like you. We had good times together."

"You wanna know the truth? I liked fighting with you. You were one of the only people that I could just hang out with, play quarters, drink like sailors, and punch in the face!"

"Exactly. And then hug each other afterwards."

"Maybe not hug each other—"

"We never held grudges," I said, trying to placate him. "We fought, we got up, and we partied together the next day."

"That's the way it's supposed to be."

"I didn't know it was your birthday. I'm sorry, and I was nervous to reach out, but I'm sure there are things you want to know."

"Like I said, I always wanted to know things you couldn't tell me. Like what time did you get to Dunkin' Donuts? I was there that night, and I screamed through the woods, asking where you all were."

"Who told you we were there?"

"Look, there are only like five places you could've been that night. Someone told me you were headed there."

"We didn't know we were going there, so how could you have known we were going there? Billy, we were walking without a plan. It was a last-minute thing. For all you know, we could've been going back to my mother's house."

"What time did you get there?" he asked again.

"I don't know. We were tripping out. But for you to say that you went there, and you were screaming—that's bullshit."

"They told me you were going there."

"No one knew we were going there!" I worried that I wasn't getting anywhere with Bill. "Do me a favor: when you get sobered up tomorrow, let's talk. I want to make sure we're on the same page."

"I'm fine. Let's keep going."

"Call me tomorrow around noon. No big deal. I don't want to get mad because you say things that piss me off. I know it's your birthday. I don't want you wondering and having remorse. I want you to be at peace, and I want you to like me. It's not fair to you to wonder what happened. I'm not looking to debate."

"Well, let's just have another conversation. I've already cracked another beer. I respected you until what happened with Gary."

"But you don't know what really happened. You'll never understand until you know the truth. I'm not a criminal."

"Promise me you'll tell me the truth tomorrow."

"I promise. I should've made a statement a long time ago. It's not right for you and the rest of our Northport family to feel guilt after all these decades. That's my mistake."

"Why do you think I let them put my quotes in that book?"

"Which book?" I snapped. "I know there was a book called *Say You Love Satan*, but I didn't read it."

"No, not that one. Anyway, it's a book of truth. *Acid King*! That's what it was called. Ninety-eight percent of it is hard truth."

"What was your statement in the book?"

"Not just me," Billy said, and I heard him take a swig of beer. "Everybody but you gave quotes for that book. The author reached out to you too."

"So everybody knows but me even though I was the one there? It's amazing how everybody knows everything, but only I had to walk the walk. I haven't even told one person what happened in thirty-eight years."

I know you're the only one who's never said anything or had an interview with anyone, by the way. I still talk to your sisters on Facebook.

"You know, Albert, Gary's mom said Gary's death killed her husband. He just died after what happened. After Gary died, I didn't cry for eight months. I was filled with rage. I found a cat that died in my arms, and Gary always loved stray cats. And then I broke down crying. I was filled with so much hate."

Billy was meandering, and I knew I had to end the call. He was too drunk.

"And I know it wasn't easy for you, either," he continued. "You lost your family. You moved out of town. You disappeared. I wish you told me you went to the service. I might've joined you."

"I would've taken you with me," I said. "I took three other friends with me."

"Gary was supposed to show up two weeks after he died. He had already been accepted to fly helicopters. He was supposed to join the air force."

"Military doesn't just say that. You have to take a test, go to school. It's a lot of procedures. First, you become an ROTC officer and go to school for four years—school, man. And then you become a lieutenant or captain. You gotta move up the rank. But forget about that. Sleep well, Billy."

"What a great birthday gift to put an end to all of this. Thank you, Albert."

Billy lied. I still don't understand how he could've known that we went to Dunkin' Donuts that night. And he said that one of the books about Gary's murder, *The Acid King*, was nearly completely correct, yet he knew that we weren't cult members. On top of that, he was wasted for our entire call. For all I know, this was just a game to him. But for me, the truth about what happened is everything.

CHAPTER 7

WILLIAM LEASON
(SECOND INTERVIEW)

I DECIDED TO call William, Billy Leason, back after all these years. He was a big part of this drama and lies that have been going around for many years. On August 27, 2021, a Tuesday, around eleven o'clock at night, I decided to pick up the phone. I picked up the phone. I dialed William, and he answered. I was going to tell him I'm proud of him that he got his life together, but as usual, he's not changed. He was very drunk and arrogant as he was in the past. He stated how he wanted to kill me ten years ago, then he asked me what happened. I said, "Billy, you and I have never had problems. All you had to do was pick up the phone and call me. Rumor has it that William ran around, making statements that he knew weren't true and he knows what really happened."

William Leason was just trying to be a social media whore. He wanted to know what really happened. He said to me, "Albert, you were the only one who stayed quiet. All those years, you're the only one who's never given an interview to anyone and wanted to know what really happened." I was quiet all these years, William, out of respect for my mother and sisters and their image. Now enough is enough. As the years went on, I've seen the stories get out of control and worse and worse every year, and you know what I'm talking about.

I knew he was nervous because he knew that I knew about the lies. It was time to grab the bull by the horns and get him to admit that he lied. I asked him a few simple questions. I needed to let him know that I was writing a story about what really happened and want his permission to put him in my book. I asked him if it would be okay to have him in my book and put photos in my book as well. He said okay to being part of my book.

EYEWITNESS

So I recorded and interviewed him, and now it was time to ask him simple questions. So I asked him, "Do you believe that this was a cult?" William said no. "Do you believe that I would do anything to harm anybody like that?" William again said no, and I said, "Do you believe that Ricky and all of us were a devil-worshipers cult?" William Leason said no. I said to him, "So why is it that you were running around, spreading all these rumors, making things worse, and hurting these people that went through enough tragedies and pain?" William Leason did not realize that I knew everything that he was spreading. He was in shock. For the first time, he was at a loss for words. I stated that he made me sick and disgusted with him, the way he spread all those lies just to be in the media. I told him I was disappointed in him, hurt, and mad at him and said he was still the same and hasn't changed. I told him he was an alcoholic and still a liar. Then I said that after all these years, William Leason hasn't changed. I hope that he finds the peace that he's looking for in my book, and I don't judge anybody. I judge people on the way they treat me, and God will judge everybody for their actions. So deep down inside,

I know that as long as I tell the truth, treat people with respect, and do the right things, I'm good in the eyes of God. And that's my interview with William.

He said no, but he would've been able to stop it. I said, "You weren't there, Billy. You have no idea what was going on.

He stated, "He went all over the place looking for us. And went to Northport Aztakea Woods looking for us."

I said to Billy, "How was it that you knew we were at Northport Aztakea Woods?"

Billy replied with, "I just had a feeling."

Albert replied back and said, "We didn't even know where we were going."

Then William Billy Leason replied and said, "He heard we went there."

Albert replied back, "And said from who?"

Billy said, "From around."

Albert replied to Billy and said, "You've never even been to the Northport Aztakea Woods."

Albert replied and said, "Did you go to the party that Sandrine had for her boyfriend, Chuck?"

Billy said, "What party?"

I said, "Oh, so you did not know about the party that was going on that night where there was at about two hundred people there?"

I said, "Really, William Billy Leason?"

Albert said, "Stop the goddamn lies, William. William Billy Leason, you know I know everything you and Ben were saying was nothing but bullshit lies all those years, and then you went off to help write a book with Jesse P. Pollack called *The Acid King*, and you told him nothing but lies. Right?"

William Billy Leason was quiet for once in his life I said, "Answer these questions, William Billy Leason, and then maybe I'll tell you what happened."

He said, "Fine."

I said, "Do you believe that I am part of the devil worshiping cult?"

Billy said no, then I said to Billy, "Do you believe that I've dug up the Indian graveyard?"

He said no, then I said to Billy, "Do you believe that I'm a cult leader and a devil worshiper?"

He said no. I said, "You know what really pisses me off? You've given a lot of statements to a lot of people, and you weren't even there. I'm disgusted with your behavior because I've never done anything to you, and for you to say that about my family and me—I'm disgusted with you, and you still haven't changed. There was many times we've gone to parties and you were so drunk that people wanted to beat you up, and I stopped them from beating you up, and I walk you down the beach, Billy! From Ricky's house I waited to the morning time for you to sober up because everyone wanted you out of the party. I put forty dollars in your pocket to send you home, so that no one was going to beat you up, Billy, and you treated me this way."

I said, "It's disgusting for a person who knows me, and you act like you know everything, but you weren't even there, and you act like you were Gary's best friend. All those times you couldn't find Gary for weeks at a time—Gary was getting sick of you, and he was hanging out at my house, going out with my sister. Did you know that?"

He said no. I said, "There's a lot of things you don't know. If I could've stopped it, I would've, but for you to talk all that, and you don't know what's going on. You make me sick, Billy. You've just admitted it—you know nothing and all your statements are lies. I've recorded you now, and you already gave me the okay and don't even realize it. How to make you understand what I went through before statements, but in reality my statement now I'm giving now is the truth because you were being recorded and let everyone expose you for what you are—a liar. When I finish writing this book, Billy, then you will know what really happened, and everyone will know what you really are about also to add that Billy had made a statement saying that he was forced out of New York to live in Houston, Texas, for stealing a police officer's radio out of a police officer's car and was pulled over for drinking, driving, and having to give up a drug dealer."

"Willam Billy Leason, shame on you, Billy." Jealousy and lies began. Social media whore, Willam Billy Leason aka Billy. I decided to call Billy up after all these years he created rumors and gossip lies to the media about me Ricky Jimmy Gary. Whatever it took for him to get in the spotlight or on any paper or any book he would do. I am left with the pains the scars of two of my friends that died and killed each other. The horrible rumors and lies that were spread. Like it was a satanic cult. Or devil worshipers that sacrifice animals that was so far from the truth. The rumor started off from one chief of police Howie That started this media frenzy with lies. Then he was forced to retract the statement but it's spun out so far out of control that the media did not want to hear the truth. it was about making a fast dollar and to this day people still spreading false rumors and making books and movies to make a dollar regardless of people life and their careers and their families. It's disgusting the way the media is and they should be all punished for false advertising and for destroying lives cruelty to let parents think and live the life thinking that it was a devil worshiping satanic cult is disgusting aka Billy and jimmy was a big part of this rumors and I interviewed Billy Leason. August 17 on around 11:30 at night Billy as usual he was drunk bragging about how he's drinking all day some people never changed still the same as he was as a kid. This was all documented and recorded and this was okayed by Willam Billy Leason because he thought I was going to give him the story that he's been looking for all these years. Sorry, Billy Willam Leason, you're not getting any story from me. I will let everyone hear your recorded interview on my web page and your confession and that you are a liar and always have been. You can read this in my book, William Billy Leason. He was from Harborfields High School. William Billy Leason came to Northport High School. A year after the incident happened to us, he graduated from Northport High School.

CHAPTER

ROBERT ATKINSON

I DECIDED TO call Robert Atkinson on August 29, 2021, at 9:00 PM. It happened to be on his wife's birthday.

Robert asked me how I had been. I told Robert I was writing a book. Robert Atkinson said, "It's about time. I think it's a good idea, Albert. It's long overdue. Albert, what can I do for you?

"How did it affect you, and what do you think about everything that's been going on with the story and social media?"

Robert said, "Albert, the media really destroyed your image and reputation, and everyone is disgusted, really disgusted, with the media and how they blew this out of proportion. And they are so far off, Albert, from what they're saying about you. I remember you being very religious and very good at sports. Even my brothers, Kenny and Steve, came home one day and said, 'Do you know that guy next-door, Albert Quinones?' I said to my brothers, 'Yes, I know him. What about him?' Kenny and Steve said, 'Do you know that guy is really good in sports?' I said to my brothers, "I already know that. Albert is a beast when it comes to playing sports. You put him in any position or anywhere in the field and unleash him, and he will win every time.'"

I remember when Kenny Atkinson's father, was a salesman and came over to my house. He introduced himself to my mother, Nancy, and he was selling Hoover vacuum cleaners. That was the first time I met Mr. Atkinson—Kenny and Robert Atkinson's father. My mother bought a vacuum cleaner from Mr. Atkinson and used the vacuum every day nonstop. She was a cleaning fanatic. I must say, growing up as kids with the Atkinson family was very competitive but fun. We would go to the beach together, and we'd play Frisbee and volleyball. Robert and Kenny Atkinson had a nice basketball court in the backyard. Kenny, Robert, and I would go to their backyard and play basketball all day and all night. We had a lot of good times.

I said to Robert, "You were like family to me, a brother I never had. If I need any advice, I would always get the best advice from you, Robert, and your brothers. This is why I am asking you if I am doing the right thing, writing this book Robert."

Robert replied, "Albert, I think you should do the book, set the record straight, and tell the world the truth for once and for all."

I remember Robert Atkinson's father used to sit in the garage and work on this old wooden station wagon in the 1930s, called a woody. His father would have to take the car and the motor apart, and it took Mr. Atkinson alone time to put it back together. Robert and I were laughing, reminiscing about the old times Robert and I had a big soccer game in the backyard when it was raining. We were so covered in mud and exhausted that when we walked into the house, Robert Atkinson's mom yelled at us because we got mud all over the house, and she told us to get out of the house.

"Robert, can you tell me a little bit more about Ricky and what you know about Ricky Kasso?"

"I remember playing football with Ricky in Northport's junior high. Ricky Kasso was very funny and goofy, and he was a nice guy. Ricky Kasso was not what the papers made him out to be. Ricky just couldn't live up to expectations that his father wanted him to be. His father was abusive and put him down all the time, but overall, Ricky was liked by most of the people in Northport. And I liked Ricky too."

"Robert, can you tell me a little bit about Jimmy Troiano? Because in most of his articles and interviews, Jimmy Troiano states how close he was to us, that he went to school in Northport, and that he was on the football team in Northport."

"Albert, I can tell you this. I never saw Jimmy Troiano ever play football, let alone saw Jimmy in our school. He came to Northport for a short time, but that was during the summer of 1984, in June, before the Ricky-Gary incident. But other than that, Albert, I've never seen Jimmy in our school, and I never saw him at any football practice or game ever or saw Jimmy playing football at all in Northport."

"Are you sure, Robert?"

Robert replied, "I would know, Albert, because I was the captain of the football team. I was there every day. Albert, look at Jimmy and his criminal track history. I think you need to write this book. The lies have been going on for too long, and it upsets me to see these people say these things about you when it's so far not you. You're a good guy, Albert. You always have been. You just ended up at the wrong place at the wrong time. And if there's anything I can do for you, please, Albert, don't hesitate to ask. I love you like a brother."

"Love you too, Robert."

"Albert, I have to cut it short. It's my wife's birthday. Please don't be a stranger, and call me anytime."

Robert Atkinson, the brother of Kenneth Atkinson the New York Brooklyn Nets' basketball coach, lives out East of Long Island Southamptons. Robert has a wife, five kids, and a good business and computers, and he is doing very well for himself.

Jimmy Troiano was never in Northport or on the Northport football team. Jimmy was not friends with us or went to the school or was on the football team, and he's constantly in trouble for robberies and many other things. Jimmy Troiano is not a very good credible witness. As you heard from Robert Atkinson, the brother of Kenny Atkinson and the NBA New York Nets's basketball coach's brother. So here you have it now—Robert Atkinson's story.

CHAPTER 9

RICHARD BARTON

I DECIDED TO call Richie Barton. It's been a long time, and we were close friends, we haven't spoken in many years. Rich Barton moved to Florida and opened up a construction company. He got married, had kids of his own, and is doing very well for himself.

"I decided to write a book, and I would like to ask you about what you went through, if it's okay with you."

"Anything I can do to help you with this. You've been through enough, Albert, and whatever I can do to put this to rest, I'm there for you."

I said, "Thank you, old friend. I'm tired of seeing all the bullshit lies that people are making up. I know that you went up to Aztakea Woods to see the dead body of Gary Lauwers. Can you tell me a little bit about what happened that day?"

RICHIE BARTON

Richie had just woken up, and his father had just come home from California. He drives an 18-wheeler tractor trailer cross county. That's how he earns his living. He was gone for about two weeks. Richie's mom was making lunch for everybody. Richie decided to call up Mark to ask him what he was doing and if he wanted come over to hang out and smoke some trees. Mark said he had just got home from work and that yes, he would come over and hang. Richie said to Mark that Ricky and Jimmy were on their way over, and I really don't like Jimmy. He gives me the creeps. Jimmy has a creepy look on his face all the time. I get bad vibes from him. Do you know what I mean?

Mark replied to Rich Barton, "I know what you mean. I have the same feeling about Jimmy. I will come over."

Mark Florimonte asked Richie, "Have you spoken to Albert?"

Richy replied, "Albert hasn't picked up his phone in a while. I don't know what's going on with him."

Mark replied, "Okay, just checking to see if he's okay."

Richy said to Mark, "I called his mom, Ms. Quinones, and she said Albert's not home. Kind of weird. I don't know why, but he's been keeping his distance."

Mark Florimonte replied to Richie Barton, "I am on my way over now. I'll see you in a little, Richy."

When Richie got off the phone with Mark, Richie Barton's mother yelled downstairs and said that Rick Kasso and Jimmy Troiano were here. Richie then told his mom, Sally Barton, to tell Jimmy and Rick to come downstairs.

Richy Barton said, "What's up, Ricky and Jimmy?"

Jimmy Troiano was being cocky and loud as usual, but Ricky Kasso was very quiet in a weird way. Ricky Kasso didn't look very happy; he looked very confused. Richie asked Ricky if he was okay, but Ricky didn't answer. Yeah, there was a sad look in his eyes—a pale zombie look—what confusion He was as not right inside; Richie could see it. Richie then went to his closet and pulled out a bong that had four tubes so all of them could smoke out of it.

Jimmy Troiano was sitting in Richie's beanbag and asked if he could play some albums of Ozzy Osbourne.

"Not a problem, Jimmy. I have two milk crates over there in corner with the records in there, and you can put on whatever album you want. Turn on the purple light while you're at it, okay?"

Then Sally Barton screamed downstairs and said, "Richie, your friend Mark is at the door!"

Richie yelled up to his mom and told her, "Tell Mark Florimonte to come downstairs, okay, Mom?"

Richy's mom said to lower the music. "Your father needs to rest. He had been on the road for two weeks, driving his 18-wheeler truck, and he needs to rest. So if you can't keep the music down, Richie, then go out and do something else."

Rich Barton replied to his mother, "Okay, we will keep it down, Mom."

Mark came down the stairs. As Rich Barton opened the door for Mark, Rich said to Mark, "What's going on with everyone? They're acting totally weird. They're not acting like themselves."

"Yeah, I know. Ricky Kasso was acting very quiet and not saying anything. That's not like him Richie said to Mark. "Well, Ricky's not talking, and he seems very confused and is acting weird. I keep asking him what's wrong, but he's not saying anything. Jimmy's in a good mood. Yeah, well, something's going on."

They all sat down and started smoking. They turned on the purple light and had Ozzy play.

Jimmy said, "Listen, Ricky, I think we should move the body," but Ricky didn't say anything. Jimmy then said, "I told a couple a couple of people what you did, and we need to move it somewhere else so they don't find it."

Mark Florimonte and Richie Barton looked at each other as if saying, "What are you talking about?"

Jimmy said to Mark and Richie, "Ricky Kasso killed Gary. Ricky and Gary were having a fight because Gary stole Ricky's money and drugs."

Mark said to Jimmy, "Bullshit, Ricky would not do that to Gary over some stupid shit like that. Ricky Kasso did not say a word. "Ricky Kasso and Gary Lauwers have been friends since elementary school, and Ricky has never had a fight in his life. It's bullshit." Ricky Kasso looked at those two then silently nodded his head up and down with a tear coming down his left eye.

Richy and Mark Florimonte looked at each other and didn't believe Jimmy or Ricky; they thought it was a gag/joke.

Ricky stood up, looked Jimmy dead in his face, and said with an angry, low tone in his voice, "Jimmy, you said you were not going to say anything to anyone, and here you are, telling everybody what happened." You could see the rage in Ricky's eyes. And for the first time, Jimmy was quiet and looked scared. Jimmy looked away with his piercing blue eyes. Jimmy couldn't look at Ricky.

"You're trying to get me in more trouble, Jimmy. It's bad enough that this happened, and now you're running around, telling everyone what I did" Ricky Kasso said to Jimmy. "Who else did you tell, Jimmy? Tell me now."

Jimmy didn't expect Ricky to say anything because Ricky was always quiet.

"Who else did you tell, god damn it!" Ricky said, "This is the last time I'm asking you, Jimmy. Who else did you tell?" he continued with anger in his voice.

Jimmy replied, "I told Laurie Walsh and my girlfriend, Karen Novollino. I don't think they believe me."

Ricky said to Jimmy, "Thanks a lot for keeping your damn mouth shut."

Mark said to Rich Barton, "I am not sure if they're telling us the truth."

Mark told Rich Barton to actually play along with it, saying, "They are really good. Let's play along with it. I don't believe them."

Jimmy said to Ricky Kasso, "We should move the body before someone finds Gary's dead body and we get caught."

Mark and Rich decided to play along and agreed to help Ricky and Jimmy move the body.

Rich Barton, to Mark, whispered, "Those two have some game going on, but we're not falling for it." And they laughed silently.

Rich said, "I have a shovel in my shed."

Mark laughed and said, "Yeah, let's go do this. Let's go, Jimmy. Show us where Gary's dead body is," and started chuckling.

They started to go up upstairs and went to the shed to grab the shovel. Richie told his mom they were going out for a little bit and would be back later for dinner.

Richie's mom said, "Dinner will be at six, and stay out of trouble," but she knew her son was hanging out with Jimmy.

Richie said, "Okay, okay, we'll be back later."

Everyone started walking up Maple Avenue and then went down Main Street, past the Midway.

Mark said, "Let's get some cigarettes from the Midway. Ziggy is working."

Jimmy said, "Good idea. I'm out of cigarettes too."

So Mark went inside the Midway and said, "Hey, how are you?" It was getting late outside, and the sun was starting to go down. It was a little damp out as if it was getting ready to rain. "Ziggy, can you grab me a pack of cigarettes?"

Ziggy said, "Sure." Ziggy then asked Mark, "Have you seen Albert? I need some weed. If you see him, let him know to stop by."

Mark replied, "When I see him, but he hasn't spoken to anyone in a while. No one knows what's going on with him, but we will let him know if we see him."

Jimmy shouted at Mark, "Let's go, Mark! What are you and Ziggy doing, going on a date?" and then laughed at Mark.

Mark said, "Yeah, funny, ha ha," then we started walking south up Laurel Avenue and past Northport's junior high and we got to 25-A. Going west passing Dunkin' Donuts and the roller-skating rink. Ricky still had not said anything.

Richy Barton said to Mark, "We'll find out soon enough if it's bullshit or not."

Mark said, "This is crazy weird. Do you think they really did it? Because now I'm starting to think they did kill Gary. What do you think?"

"Mark, I don't know."

Mark said, "I am starting to think they did."

Jimmy turned around and said, "We're almost there. We just have to go past the Italian restaurant Robske's where Albert works." Then Jimmy said to Mark, "Can we get some hamburgers on the way?"

Mark replied to Jimmy, "I don't think so, Jimmy."

They made a right off 25-A Street, going north on Church Street for a block, and we made a left on Franklin Street going westbound and started walking up to the path. They smelled a really bad smell, like something was rotten—like a dead animal. The closer they got to the path the stronger the smell got. It was so bad. Mark and Richie took their shirts and covered their mouths and noses. They wanted to know if this was true or not. They kept walking on the path. When got to the site, yeah, they saw the dead body of their friend. The body was so decomposed that half of it was covered in maggots.

The eyes were stabbed out of the head, and the body was so decomposed. They weren't even thinking about moving it. They wanted to get the hell out of the woods as fast as possible. The odor was so overwhelming that they were choking.

The body was in the sun, causing the body to decompose faster than ever. It was very surprising that the neighbors didn't complain about the odor or investigate where that odor was coming from in an upscale, rich suburban area. They rushed to get out of the woods, gagging and gasping for fresh air, running down the trail onto the main street, choking, throwing up, and spitting out that taste from their mouths. They finally started getting some fresh oxygen. And in shock they were.

Jimmy started to laugh. "I told you. I told you, Mark," Jimmy said as he laughed at Mark and Richie Barton as they were spitting out the nasty taste from their mouths.

Mark and Richie Barton were in shock that that it was true. Their friend Ricky Kasso killed their friend Gary Lauwers. Jimmy said they had to leave the woods and that there was nothing they could do about it now.

They started walking back to Richie Barton's house. Ricky Kasso was sick to his stomach, and the rest were in shock. The friend that they grew up with killed another friend that they grew up with. They were at a loss for words and felt all over the place as well. No one thought it was funny except for Jimmy. They all walked back home, and as they got up to Dunkin' Donuts, Mark Florimonte said to everyone that he had to go home now since it was getting late and his mom was making dinner. Mark walked past Richie Barton and whispered to Richie, "You need to get away from them guys, and don't let Jimmy and Kasso go back to your house." Richie nodded his head slightly up and down, agreeing with Mark.

Ricky, Jimmy, and Rich Barton started walking to Rich Barton's home. As they walked past Northport's junior high school, they started walking down Main Street and got to the Midway's smoke shops. That's when Richie Barton said to Jimmy and Rick Kasso, "My dad just came home from California, and it's getting kind of late. I have to go home, have dinner, and spend time with my father." Rich Barton said to Ricky Kasso and Jimmy, "I will talk to you guys later. I have to go home, spend time with my dad, and eat dinner."

"Okay," they replied, "no problem." And they walked off into a different direction. Richie had no idea where they went, and as he was walking home, he said to himself, "Now I know why Albert's keeping his distance and not saying anything to anyone. Albert must be losing his mind right now."

Richie couldn't believe this happened; they were all good friends and grew up together. He know Jimmy had something to do with this. Ricky Kasso would never do that to anyone. All this shit did not start until Jimmy came to Northport. Ricky Kasso was always the quiet and goofy kid.

ALBERT

Richie said, "The reporters were all over my house. We couldn't even get out of the house. It was so crazy, Albert. I saw the reporters on your porch, knocking on your doors and windows, Albert, and they were all over my door too. I felt bad for you. I wanted to come over, but my mother wouldn't let me out of the house. I saw all the lights from the news station vans' spotlights all over your house. I was sick to my stomach. I can't imagine what you were going through just for being at the wrong place at the wrong time. They demolished you, and you didn't do anything or were even arrested for anything, Albert.

We had it bad, but you had it worse than any of us. I'm sorry you had to go through that, Albert."

"Richie, you've been a good friend. It wasn't easy for me to see two of my friends die and to see all you guys go through this. I didn't tell you what they did because I didn't want you to be harassed and interrogated. The less you guys knew the better. I remember coming to your house, and you had a *Rolling Stone* journalist there. I was shocked that you were sitting there with him, Rich Barton, because I did not tell you or anyone what happened that night. I was not happy. I was pretty pissed to see that I didn't tell you to protect you Richy Barton, but when I saw the guy from *Rolling Stone*, I figured maybe I should just let everyone know what happened because the DA was trying to make me lie. I figured that would be the best way for everyone to know, but then my mother came walking in and yelled at your mom, Sally Barton, before I could say anything to *Rolling Stone* journalist. As soon as I got home, Mom called the DA, William Keaton, to let him know that *Rolling Stone* was trying to interview me, and that's when they agreed to send me to Georgia. It was because I was under a lot of stress. Every reporter was trying to get a story from me. I was the only one who kept my mouth shut, but it was your friendship and everyone else that helped me get through this. And I appreciate you guys for helping me, being there for me, and not judging me based on the crap you hear on the streets. I just want you to know that, Rich Barton, and thank you. You're like a brother to me, and I'll always be there for you anytime you need me. So there you have it. That's my story."

CHAPTER 10
MARK FLORIMONTE

APRIL 29, 10:00 P.M.

Mark Florimonte

ALBERT QUINONES

I CALLED MARK. It was just like old times, as if we were never apart. It's been forty years. Whenever we had a problem, we would talk. I told Mark I was going to write a book about what happened to us in Northport and asked if he could tell me what he remembered.

Mark Florimonte replied, "I would be happy to help you do this book, Albert. It was the weekend, and I came over to your house, Albert, to hang out with Richie Barton and Wendy.

"We were drinking beer, and we were smoking weed and having a good time. I was doing some cocaine. I asked you what was wrong, Albert, and you replied, 'I'll tell you what's wrong, but I'm not telling you everything. Ricky Kasso killed Gary. Ricky Kasso killed Gary a week ago, but the less you know the better off you guys are.' Mark and Richie replied that Jimmy had taken them to see the body. Shortly after that, a knock was at the door. The cop asked if Albert was here."

*****

EYEWITNESS

On that day, I came out of the bathroom. I walked up to the cops and said to the blue-and-white cop, "What's up?"

I went outside with Mark, and the cop asked me if I would back him up. The cop had a call saying there was a house being robbed. I knew that was bullshit.

"Albert, can you just come with me, sit in the car, and back me up if I need you?"

I replied, "Yes, I would go."

When I left that night with the cops, I left the house, and as we drove off in the cop car down Maple Avenue, three undercover cars pulled around the blue-and-white car, and three men in black suits pulled me out of the cop's car, said, "Albert, come with us," grabbed me, and pushed me into a black undercover. I knew shit was going down now. There was not one word sad said in the car, but they knew what happened to Gary. The detectives drove down Motor Parkway. I was pulled behind the court building. It was late. It was after midnight. There was no one at the court building for us. We went through the door and up two flights of stairs into a room with one chair and floodlights. They sat me in the chair and started asking me questions about what happened to

Gary, where Gary was, who killed him, and who else was with me when Gary was killed.

I was beaten for four and a half hours by the undercover detectives with police batons and phone books.

I was told to stand in front of the wall and spread my arms and legs as they kicked me in my testicles many times, throwing cups of water into my face many times through the night.

After four and a half hours, the detective said, "I don't think the guy knows anything. No one can take a beating like that and not talk." The detective then said, "Let's drop him back at his house. If we need him, we can always pick him back up." So they dropped me off at my home.

When I walked in the house, everyone asked where I had been. I told Mark and Rich that I was beaten and asked about Gary. I told them I did not say anything to the cops. "I can't tell you everything. The less you know the better it is for you guys. It's for your own good, trust me. Mark, Richy Barton, you don't wanna know."

I told Mark and Rich Barton they should just go home because I knew the police were coming back. It was going to be a shit show, and I did not want Mark and Richie to be in the middle of this nightmare.

Mark and Rich Barton replied, "We're not going to leave you, Albert."

I told Mark and Richie that I was going down to the docks in Northport and go fishing, and I said, "Let them pick us up there. I don't want the cops to kick my mom's door down in front of all my neighbors."

I called my mom, telling her I was going fishing at the Northport docks. So Mark, Richie Barton, and I headed toward the Northport docks with three fishing poles and a bucket, and we started fishing. Three hours later, we saw the cops driving down Main Street. It looked like a giant Christmas tree with all the lights flashing off and on. The police drove up to the docks. They pulled their guns out and started running down the docks with their guns drawn out, telling us to put our hands up in the air. They separated all three of us and placed each of us in different cars. Then they drove us back to the Northport police station to interrogate us.

The police brought me into a room, sat me down, and told me to tell them the truth. They said that they had Ricky and Jimmy in another room. I stuck with the same story, saying that I didn't know anything.

"Ricky told us you had nothing to do with it."

I told the cops I didn't know what they were talking about.

Detective Jean Roma said he was going to bring Ricky Kasso back into the room to prove to me they had him. They walked Ricky into my room. And I saw Ricky. He had a tear go down his face.

Ricky confessed and said, "I told him I did it, Albert, and you had nothing to do with it. Tell your mom I love her, and I'm sorry. I never meant for this to happen."

I started to cry as they took Ricky Kasso away—a sign of relief from not knowing whether they were going to pin it on me or if they were going to take responsibility for what happened. I was relieved that Ricky took full responsibility for this.

The cops took Ricky away into another room. They came back into my room and said they would give me immunity if I told them what happened. Then I would be able to leave and go home. I wrote them a statement. The DA said they wanted Jimmy to go down for it to and made another statement, and they then told me that if I didn't sign it, I would not get immunity and would not go home. They said that if I signed it and agreed to the terms, I would be the state witness, and if I did not sign the statement then I'll go to jail with Jimmy as an accomplice. Rumor has it that Jimmy had taken his father's handgun and carjacked a car to go upstate to Saratoga, only to find out it was a district attorney's car from Suffolk County's court district. I signed the form that they wanted me to but did not feel good about it Officer Jean Roma a friend of the family had told me to sign it and promised he would take me home. Police officer Jean Roma then took off the handcuffs, walked me out the back the police station, put me in the car, and drove me to my mother's house. When we arrived, he knocked on the door and told my mom, "Your son Albert was involved in a murder but did not have anything to do with it, but he was there. And so what happened was that he was at the wrong place at the wrong time, and I'm sorry to tell you this, Nancy."

My mother was in complete shock. I did not know what to say. She didn't ask if I was okay and didn't ask what happened. No one spoke about it. I was left to figure it out on my own.

*****

"Thank you, Mark, for talking to me," I said to Mark Florimonte.

And Mark said, "Thank you too, Albert, for telling me what you had to go through, and I'm sorry you had to go through that alone Albert and if there is anything else I can do just ask me. I'm here for you too, Albert."

CHAPTER 11

KAREN NOVELLINO— JIMMY'S GIRLFRIEND

I DECIDED TO rent a car and go out to Northport to see Karen. It was a lovely day out, not a cloud in the sky. I drove through Main Street, Northport, and saw Karen coming out of Phase Two Pizza Place. I pulled over and said, "Karen, I was just coming to see you."

Karen said, "Really, Albert? What about?"

I said, "I decided to write a book to get the truth out once and for all to stop all the lies that have been flying around for years."

Karen said, "That's great, Albert. It's about time we get to the bottom of this. What can I do for you, Albert? You look great, by the way. Thank you, Karen Novellino."

"I was wondering if you could tell me what you know about what happened and your experience."

"Well, I don't know where to start, but I was home, bored, nothing to do, and I decided to call Laurie Walsh and see what she was doing. I called Laurie and asked Laurie what she was doing, and she said that she was going to the mall to get some bathing suits, and she was having a barbecue at her house. Lori asked me if I would like to go shopping with her. Her father was coming home from work, and he was going to drop us both off at Smith Haven Mall."

KAREN NOVOLLINO

Karen said "Sure, I'll be more than happy to go with you, Laurie. I'll see you in about ten minutes." Karen got ready and headed to Laurie's house, and when she got to Laurie's house and knocked on the door, Laurie's father answered the door. He was in his police uniform, and Karen asked him if Laurie was home.

Mr. Walsh called Lori downstairs and said, "Your friend Karen is down here." Her father ask Karen and Laurie if they were ready to go to the mall, and they replied yes. Laurie's father drove Karen and Laurie from Northport to a mall where they could go shopping for bathing suits. An hour later, Laurie's father went back to the mall to pick them up and take them back to Laurie's house, where Laurie's father and mother prepared a barbecue for everyone.

It was a nice day out for a barbecue. It wasn't too hot, and it wasn't too cold. There was not a cloud in the sky. It was a perfect day until Jimmy was looking for Karen all over the place. Jimmy went over to the side gate of Laurie's house and saw Laurie and Karen.

Laurie said to Jimmy, "You know you're not allowed over here. My father doesn't want you over, Jimmy."

Jimmy replied, "It's very important, Karen."

Karen replied, "What's up, Jimmy?"

Jimmy replied, "I'm on my way upstate with Ricky, Karen. I just wanted to see you, and you'll never believe what happened. Ricky killed Garry."

Laurie said, "Bullshit, we don't believe you, Jimmy."

Jimmy replied, "Do you want to see the body? I took a few people up there already, but you have to promise not to tell anyone."

Karen and Laurie said, "No, we can't. We're having a barbecue. You have to go now, Jimmy."

"I'll call you later, Karen."

Laurie said to Karen, "What do you see in Jimmy?"

Karen replied, "I don't know. I think it's the 'bad boy' look."

Lori and Karen decided to call Gary's mother because they were very disturbed about what Jimmy said. Karen and Laurie called Gary's mother, and she said she had not seen Gary in over a week. "Laurie, if you see Gary, please tell Gary to call home. We're very worried about him."

Lori said, "If we see Gary, we will let you know and tell him to call home."

Laurie and Karen knew this wasn't a joke. They decided to go down to Northport Park. It was a crystal clear night, and there was not a cloud in the sky. Everybody was in the park, hanging out as usual.

EYEWITNESS

Karen and Laurie asked around if anyone had seen Gary. Everyone they asked said they had not seen Gary in over a week. Laurie and Karen started to worry and believed Jimmy was telling the truth for once in his life.

Karen went back to Laurie's house. Laurie told her father, who was a police officer, that Jimmy told her and Karen that Ricky killed Gary in the Northport Aztakea Woods and Albert and Jimmy was there when Ricky killed Gary. Laurie Walsh told her father, who was a police officer, and he contacted Robert Howard, the chief of Northport Village's police department, and informed him what Karen and his daughter, Laurie Walsh, said That's what Jimmy Troiano, told them—that Ricky killed Gary and in the Northport Aztakea Woods. Robert Howard, the chief of police, called Officer Jean Roma and told him to investigate what he heard from Laurie Walsh and Karen Novollino. The police investigated and found out Gary Lauwers was killed and his body left in the woods, half decomposed. The police crime scene investigation team and cadaver-sniffing dogs were all over the woods, and the crime scene was all taped off. The statement Jimmy told Laurie and

Karen was true; Jimmy and Ricky were on their way back to Northport from upstate, and by now, all hell had broken loose.

Ricky and Jimmy had no idea what they were about to walk into. Ricky had no idea that Jimmy went to Laurie's house to tell Karen what Ricky did to Gary. Albert was picked up shortly after that and was beaten for four and a half hours. Albert was released because he still didn't give a statement. They weren't 100 percent certain whether Albert was involved or not. They were looking for Ricky Kasso and Jimmy Troiano. Rumor had it that Jimmy and Ricky were driving back from upstate in a stolen car that Jimmy took at gunpoint from somebody that lived in Northport and worked at central Slip court criminal building as a district attorney. Early the next morning, Jimmy and Ricky arrived at Northport, pulled the car around the block behind the Midway, and parked the car. They were exhausted from the long drive. Jimmy went to the payphone to call his girlfriend, Karen, and tell her that he and Ricky were back from upstate, that they were getting ready to take off to California, and that it was over between him and Karen. Karen replied, "Oh, really?" Then

Jimmy hung up on Karen. (Author's comment: Bad move again, Jimmy.)

Karen stated to me, the author, in clear words, "I'll help Jimmy and Ricky get caught." Karen then called Northport's police department to inform them that Jimmy and Ricky were in a station wagon behind Midway off Main Street in the early morning at around 6:00 AM. It was a wet, drizzly morning, and Ricky was sleeping in the car when the cops pulled up to arrest them. The media was all over the town like wildfire. They were at the Northport police department. Karen said the reporters camped outside her house day and night. Light from news van's spotlights flooded her house to where she could not sleep. Karen's mother kept her on tranquilizers to keep her calm. The reporters followed Karen around everywhere she went. She was on the verge of having a breakdown. Karen said she remembers riding her bicycle to the store with her friend, and the reporters were chasing them like a pack of wolves. Karen and her friend got off their bikes and ran into the store. People were staring a Karen, and a friend pointed at Karen, saying, "That's the girl, Karen, that went out with the murderer who killed Gary. Jimmy Troiano's girlfriend said, "It was a nightmare. It was like the paparazzi was after us. Karen's parents decided to relocate Karen to a different school for the year. It was way too stressful for Karen to be in Northport that year.

ALBERT

That's her story. Karen still lives in Long Island but moved to Huntington—two towns away from Northport—and is doing very well for herself.

CHAPTER 12

CHARACTER AND CREDIBILITY OF ROBERT HOWARD (NORTHPORT CHIEF OF POLICE)

TWENTY YEAR AS chief, Bob investigated one of the most notorious murder cases in local history, that of sixteen-year-old Gary Lauwers, who was killed in 1984 by Ricky Kasso and accomplice Jimmy Troiano in the Northport Aztakea Woods. The chief of the Northport police Robert Howard's kids did an interview and said that their dad always told them that all that was, was three druggies fighting over money. Peter said, "There was no real satanic murder. One guy stole somebody else's drugs, and the other guy killed him."

There you have it from the chief of police Howie's kids—what his farther, Ben, was telling. There was no satanic cult. It was put on the front page of the papers. Fact: the chief of police created this media circus and was forced to retract the statement that it was not a cult. The chief of police died on December 28, 2011. Howie's kids had made a statement saying that their father always said it had nothing to do with a cult and that it had to do with a bunch of kids on drugs who killed each other over money and drugs. Rumor has it that Robert Howard, the chief of Northport's police, was of questionable character. Rumor has it that he would have police officers beat people up to get information on who was doing what in the village of Northport. I know because I was one of them. Rumor also has it that Robert Howie, the chief of Northport's police, was also a hacker. Howie got into some serious trouble form hacking into the police database.

Howie had a good friend. His name was Jim Ruck. Jim Ruck was also very good friends with the

Atkinson family. Jim Ruck was also a coach for the Sachem school district and coached football, soccer, baseball, and basketball teams. He also coached Robert, Kenny, and Steven Atkinson. Jim Ruck was a good friend of the Atkinson family. Jim Ruck was a superintendent at the Sachem school district. Jim Ruck went to Howie to dig up information on Bob because Bob was trying to steal Jim Ruck's job as a superintendent at Sachem High School. Howie broke into the computer database at the Northport police department to dig up dirt on Bob to prevent him from taking Jim Ruck's job as a superintendent. Bob hired lawyers and investigators to find out how they got the information. They did later on find out that Howie had broken into the police database to prevent Bob from becoming the superintendent, which destroyed his name and reputation. Robert Howard was forced to resign as the chief of police in Northport.

The chief of police of Northport slandering and destroying Bob's name and credibility—that was what Robert Atkinson informed me of. So is this the type of person people would actually want to believe in and trust to protect and serve them. The chief of police of Northport was forced to resign early and kept his pension. Robert Howard has destroyed many lives and not only my life with his lies to get his name in fame. That's my interview with Robert Atkinson.

Eric Naiburg was a very young lawyer fresh out of law school and who is now in the focus in the eyes of the world. He is now Jimmy Troiano's attorney, now located in Smithtown, Suffolk County, off Motor Parkway. Eric Naiburg is desperate and willing to make his name known at any cost.

He is willing to do anything like destroy people's lives and slander people's name—just like Howie's—for the name and fame. During the day of the trial, I had to make an executive decision. Should I go with the lies that the DA wanted me to say and hang Jimmy Troiano, an innocent man, for something Jimmy didn't do? Maybe I should've. Jimmy wouldn't be spreading so many lies, as he is now) for his name, fame, and money.

I had gone onto the stand and decided to tell the truth, but the judge wanted to know why my written statement was different from my statement on the stand. I replied, "The DA wanted me to lie to put Jimmy in jail, and I refuse to live with that on my conscience." Albert's statement exonerated Jimmy Troiano of all charges. It should have ended that day. That trial should've stopped that day and never continued, but Eric Naiburg kept it going on for his name and fame. I was never arrested or prosecuted for perjury because I told the truth. Yes, after that, Eric Naiburg got another case with Amy Fisher and Joey Buttafuoco. Eric Naiburg mislead his client and had sexual relations with her. Amy Fisher stated that Eric Naiburg, her lawyer, lied to her just to have sex with her. He told Amy Fisher that if she had sex with him, she would not go to jail. Eric Naiburg was no longer allowed to represent her, and as time went on, rumor has it he was barred from practicing law. People can research it. It's in newspaper articles to this day. Is that someone you could believe and trust in their word? And is he a man you want around your kids?

This is the character and credibility of Eric Naiburg, an attorney-at-law.

> Richard LaBert—private lawyer
> for Albert Quinones (June 1984)

ALBERT QUINONES

I had a private lawyer that no one knew about, and his name is Richard LiBert, he was overseeing the illegal things that the DA, William Keaton, was doing to Albert Quinones.

The district attorney was trying to get me to tell lie, saying that Jimmy did more then what he did. The DA coached me and rehearsed with me for weeks, trying to create a massive lie, saying that Jimmy held Gary down and inventing a reason why Ricky Kasso stabbed Gary. And I didn't feel comfortable lying in court because it was a false statement, and if I refused to say what the DA wanted me say, he would have made me an accomplice to the murder and lock me up with Jimmy Troiano for murder. The district attorney's attempt was to get me to put Jimmy in jail for something he didn't do then lock me up for perjury for fifteen years.

My opinion is that Eric Naiburg was already on the same page with the DA, William Keaton, and that's what their plan was: two hit two birds with one stone.

I was confused and did not know which way to turn. I told the truth on the stand, and the DA was mad as hell and embarrassed.

I went to see my old private lawyer, Richard Libert, in person in Garden City, New York.

I want to thank Richard for not putting his name out there for fame and lying like everyone.

During my interview with Richard, my private attorney confirmed that Erick Naiburg and the district attorney William "Billy" Keaton. were out to screw me for fame in the media.

And I want to thank Richard Libert, my private attorney, for his help and, after all these years, knowing that the district attorney William Keaton and Eric Naiburg were trying to set me up. And I did the right thing, telling the truth on the stand. And thank you very, very much from the bottom of my heart, Richard Libert.

CHAPTER 13
CLOSURE

AS A KID GROWING UP IN NORTHPORT

Northport Park

EYEWITNESS

Northport was a beautiful area with old Victorian houses. It had very well-groomed properties. Most of the people that lived there were lawyers, doctors, and business owners.

There was a beautiful harbor that had boats and a dock that people would walk on, and there was a park where bands played every weekend. It was a very beautiful upbringing. Life next to my house on Lewis Road was the sandpit—a big indentation in the ground that went down half a mile. Down the hill, there was a beach called Northport Beach Eatons Neck Beach. There were also other condos and houses by the sandpit. The Northport police station had a shooting range down in the sandpit, where they had target practice.

Police from Northport would go there on the weekends to do target practice. At the bottom of the sandpit and to the right side was the Northport Fire Department's obstacle course, where they were trained, and every year, they would have the Northport Fireman's Fare, which had rides, games, gambling, and drinking that lasted for about two weeks. People used to hang glide off the cliff of the sandpit. It was beautiful to see in the morning time.

In the afternoon, I would sit on the side of the cliff to watch all the people hang glide. There were all different types and colors of hang gliders that people would fly. It was a beautiful area. Anytime I was upset or stressed, I would go to the side of the sandpit cliff and watch everyone hang glide. It took my mind off whatever I was upset about.

I went to Ocean Avenue Elementary School. My sisters Debbie and Wendy and I were all one year apart. My teacher was Mrs. Miller.

On the first day of going to school, we had to walk to school. It was it was sunny and nice outside. The walk was fairly close. I was new to Northport and was kind of nervous about going to school since my family had just moved from Cormack to Northport to start off a new life.

My mother was a home health aide nurse. And my father was in construction. My mother was a strong Irish woman 100 percent with black hair and blue eyes. My father was from Spain and part Italian—50 percent Spanish and 50 percent Italian. My mother and father had an argument, we knew.

The following day, we had to wake up to go to school—Debbie, Wendy, and I. It was a typical morning; everyone was arguing to get into the bathroom. It got to the point where I was always the last one to get into the bathroom, so I got a bucket with warm water. I filled it up at the sink, and I had a toothbrush and toothpaste in my room. I would wash up in my bedroom and piss out the back door. That was the only way I could make it to school on time.

Mom had lunch made for us. Our lunch was a ham and cheese sandwich, a bag of potato chips, and fruit punch, all in the brown paper bags sitting on the counter. As we walked out the door to school, Mom handed us a bag each.

When I got to school, the teachers at the door were helping everyone find their classes. One of the teachers grabbed one of my classroom sheets and said, "Albert, your teacher is Mrs. Miller. Your classroom is down the hall to the right, classroom 203."

I walked to the classroom. I sat down at my desk. I sat at the back of the classroom, hoping that no one would notice that I was there. But I was the first one she picked out in the classroom. Mrs. Miller asked me to stand up and introduce myself to everyone. I was nervous as hell and said, "I'm Albert. I just moved here, and I live on Lewis Road and came from

ALBERT QUINONES

Cormack." My hands were sweating so badly that I had to wipe them off on my pants. That was first time I've ever been put on the spot like that.

When lunchtime came around, that's when I met Ricky Kasso and Gary Lauwers for the first time. That's when Mark Florimonte, Rich Barton, Philip Morelli, and I became very close friends with them.

In Northport Ocean Avenue Elementary School, we had a thing called field day, and we would compete in games and field exercises and team up to see who would win in the games. It was Ricky and Gary who paired up, then it was me, Mark, and Phil Morel. And Rich Barton was paired up with teens.

Ricky Kasso, Albert Quinones, and Gary Lauwers with classmates—Elementary School—Ocean Avenue Northport

I remember one of the games was a three-legged race. Ricky and Gary would always win as a team.

Another game was the flag relay, where Mark and Albert would be in a team and would always win. We also had a game called the fifty-yard dash. Gary was very fast and always won. It made our bond stronger as friends. Gary was a very fast young kid we also had hurdle jumps and a disk-throwing contest.

Every Sunday, Mom would wake us up early to have breakfast, and we had to go to church—Debbie, Wendy, me, Mom, and Dad. Mom had a good friend named Linda Darty, and her husband, David, was a pastor. And Linda had two kids: David Junior and Peter. We'd go to church with them every Sunday in the Upper Room Tabernacle in Deer Park. The time was great; we had BMX racing bikes, Huffy bikes, and the Schwinn bikes. Ricky, Gary, Mark, and I would race our bikes through the trails in the woods. We would ride all over the place through the parks, down to the beach, and through the local trails. We were unstoppable little kids. After riding our bikes through the local trails and all over the place, Mark, Ricky, Gary, and I would go to my house, sit down, eat, talk, and laugh. Life was as good as it could get. Gary, Ricky, and I joined the soccer team. We were in the Northport Cow Harbor soccer team. Gary played goalie, I was center field, and Ricky was left wing. We worked well together as a team and won most of our games.

In the last year of elementary school, my mother and father began to have lots of arguments. My father was with another woman named Alma who we had three girls with my father before he met my mother. My father had three sisters—Migdalia, Slyvia, and Frances. My father sister Migdalia named her firstborn child Nancy Martinez after my mother's name—Nancy. My mother did not like him seeing the kids and his ex-girlfriend. They began fighting a lot, and my mother kicked him out of the house.

That's when things became very hard, but it was very confusing for me. And Mom never talked about it to us.

My father was everything to me. At least at that time, my sisters were very quiet. They were more or less on my mother's side no matter what my mother did. They were there for my mother, and she could do no wrong to them. As a kid, I think my mother took her anger out on me because of my father. I was too much like my father in many ways. That made her resent me and still to this day. She played a lot of silent-treatment games on me, and no matter what I did, I was always wrong even though I was right. It seemed like I spent most of my life as a kid saying sorry, sorry, sorry. I remember most of the time, I'd be in my room by myself, crying because I felt like she didn't love me.

Later on, my grandmother moved in because my mother was working a lot, so my grandmother watched over us. While my mother was working, Grandmother moved downstairs into the basement. She had her own room—the whole basement—with a sliding glass back door with one dog, which was a Chihuahua named Taco. My mother had come home from work, and I was downstairs with my grandmother.

Then my father came over one day on the weekend to see my mother, and then they had a fight about my father coming over again. She threw him out of the house, telling him he would never see his son Albert ever again as long as he was alive, and that went for his side of the family too. My mother kept her promise; my father had died and never got to meet me again. I know he's there in spirit. That keeps me going. I was mad and hurt because I loved my cousins and my grandmother on my father's side of the family, and that was all I ever wanted from anyone. They were part of my life and my all in my life, and it killed me to lose them. Back then, we didn't have Google or the Internet, so if you lost the phone number, you had to look it up in the phone book. And if they weren't listed, you weren't getting the phone number. Everything was found by phone books and maps—paper. I had my grandmother and my cousin on my mother's side of the family.

The school year was almost over. I remembered my grandmother was my heart. My sisters Debbie and Wendy spent most of the time upstairs when Mom was around, but I spent most of my time with Grandma downstairs. We'd stay up late and watch *The Honeymooners* and *Star Trek* at eleven o'clock. Mom would come home and tell us we all had to go to bed then argue with my grandmother.

My mom had sisters; their names are Laurie, Lisa, and Arlene. Arlene and Laurie were very close to me, and they felt bad for me because my mother was taking her anger out on me over my father. They would tell my mother to stop picking on me because I was just a kid.

EYEWITNESS

I was going out with a girl named Terry. Her father was the coach of the New York Jets. Terry was this beautiful girl with long blond hair and blue eyes. She was tall, and she was one of my best friends. She knew everything I was going through. She wanted to cheer me up, and Terry had asked her father if Joe Namath from the New York Jets could come to our class and introduce himself to me to cheer me up.

The next day, Joe Namath came to our classroom, and he introduced himself as Joe Namath and gave me a signed/autographed photo of himself. And he told me that everything would get better in life; I just had to be strong, and I could get through anything.

Then Terry looked at me with her deep crystal-blue eyes and long blond hair, and her smile made me feel better inside. It was kind of funny because she brought him in like he was a class pet or a show-and-tell class project, but deep down inside, I thought it was pretty cool. As a kid, shortly after that, I never saw Terry again; her father was transferred to the Miami Dolphins.

That was one of my first loved and heartbreaks. The next day, my mom sisters Lisa and Laurie came over to watch Debbie, Wendy, and I while my mother worked. We went down to Northport Park to play and grabbed something to eat.

Laurie and Lisa would help us do our homework. Things were looking good again as a family. Laurie and Lisa were like a second mom to all of us, and my grandmother was my love.

Every night, I would go downstairs while Grandma was watching TV. I would curl up next to Grandma and put my head on her lap. She would rub my head till I fell asleep, then she would pick me up, carry me to my bedroom, and tuck me into bed.

Elementary school was over, and we were just starting middle school. Things were getting better, and everything was becoming normal again until one day, when I came home from school, I saw my grandma getting into Aunt Lisa, Arlene, and Lauren's car. I knew that was not a good thing. My heart started racing. I just started running to my grandmother and Lisa. Before I could ask what was going on, they drove off.

I went downstairs to see what was going on, and everything my Grandma owned was gone. All I wanted to do was cry. I fell to my knees in shock and punched the floor. She had been asked to leave the house. My mother had an argument with Grandma about something. To this day, I still don't know what it was about. At that point, I had more anger than you could imagine. You could see the fire burning in my eyes with. I was angry that the only ones left who loved me were taken from my life again—my father, my grandmother, my cousins, and my aunts on both sides of the family. And now I had nobody in my life to show me love. Within a year or two, everything I had ever cared for and loved was ripped away from me. I was not allowed to talk to either side of the family. I had no contacts, no numbers, and no way to get in touch with anyone. My mother decided to move my sisters and I from Lewis Road to Maple Avenue. My mother's best friend was Beverly Bruno. Beverly Bruno said to my mother, "Nancy, you and your kids can have the keys and stay in my mother's house and rent it." That's where we lived—85 Maple Avenue, Northport.

The following day, Beverly met Nancy at 85 Maple Avenue and gave Nancy the keys to her mother's house to rent it to my mother.

My next-door neighbor was Robert Atkinson, who had brothers named Kenny and Steve Atkinson.

ALBERT QUINONES

Kenny Atkinson is actually the New York Nets NBA coach. Mr. Atkinson came over to my house as we were moving in. Mr. Atkinson introduced himself to my mother, Nancy, and ask her if she needed a Hoover vacuum cleaner. (He was a salesman for Hoover.) My mother bought a vacuum cleaner from Mr. Atkinson at $500 back then. That was the going price, and everyone had one. So my mother bought one. She vacuumed everything; curtains, floors, whatever could be vacuumed, she would vacuum it from sunrise to sunset. My mother made everyone crazy first thing in the morning; all you could hear was a vacuum going. When I was sleeping, I'd hear the vacuum in my sleep. I wanted to take that damn vacuum cleaner and throw it out the window into the garbage.

I met Robert Atkinson; he was from Northport, lived across the street from my house, and played basketball. I started playing baseball with Robert, Kenny, and Steven Atkinson. Robert Atkinson was impressed with me and how I played sports, and we became very good friends

Mr. Atkinson used to work on an old wooden car in his garage. He would take the car apart and forget how to put it back together. It would sit there for a while before he got the car back together.

Mr. Atkinson would go through boxes of parts, trying to put the car back together. He would read the manual books on how to put the motor back together. He had a lot of determination, and he got the car back together. He was a good man that never gave up and a good family man.

My two sisters—Debbie and Wendy—played volleyball and soccer. They were on the team for Northport. Debbie and Wendy were also on the cheerleading team with Laurie Walsh, who was the captain of the cheerleading team. They became good friends. Wendy and Debbie were very good friends with all the girls in school. They were pretty popular. Their friends used to come over to the house all the time, so I knew all their friends, and they knew all my friends as well.

This was where my life became confusing and complicated. At this time, I was a young boy who lost his father, and my mother was always for women's rights, women's liberty, women stick together. My mother and father split up and I don't think she ever took her anger out on him. Subconsciously, she took her anger out on me through neglect and silent treatments, making me feel unwanted.

As a parent, your job is to love your kids, be fair to your kids, and teach your kids right from wrong, not favor your kids one from another or play the kids against one another, which was what my mother did to all of us.

When I was in the eighth grade, I was diagnosed with a thing called dyslexia, which made my time in school difficult. I was sent to a Middleville junior high school since they had better programs for people that have dyslexia in that school To teach me deal with dyslexia. While Mom was driving us to school one day, I told Mom to let me off down the road from the school. I walked the rest of the way because I did not want people to see my mother driving me to school. As I was walking down Middleville Road, I looked up at the woods. There was this kid in the woods who was smoking weed. The kid asked me if I was new in the school. I replied yes. The kid replied and said his name was Mark Fite and asked me if I'd like to come up, hang out, and smoke some weed. I replied, "Sure, why not before we go to school?"

EYEWITNESS

Before we knew it, the time flew by so fast that we were a couple of hours late for school. We were so high that we started laughing, and we weren't about to make it to school. And we were only one block away from the school.

I suggested to Mark that we should go back to my house because my mother was working, and we started heading to my house, where we had chocolate chip cookies and milk and sat around, watching TV with our feet up on the coffee table, getting to know each other, becoming good friends, and smoking more weed. It was new to me, and I was starting to enjoy being stoned. It kept my mind off my parents and everybody else as well as all my problems.

It was a good feeling to be stoned until reality came into play. The school called my mother and told her I wasn't in school. When mom came home, she started yelling at me. The next day, I went to school. And Mom drove me and made sure I was there in school, where I was streaming from class to class. It was where I met a lot of people, but at the end of the day, I knew my real friends were Ricky Kasso, Gary Lauwers, Mark Florimonte, Rich Barton. They were my real friends.

Rich Barton's father was a truck driver and came home with a whole bunch of fireworks from South Carolina. We felt like we were untouchable kids. The following day. Richie and I decided to raise hell. We had two cans, and we filled the cans with bottle rockets then twisted a long fuse, connecting it to all the bottle rockets. In each can were about fifty bottle rockets. We started walking down the hallway of the school and lit the fuse to the bottle rockets, shooting bottle rockets during class hours. The kids and teachers started hiding underneath the desks as Richy Barton and I were laughing, but now, as I look back, I don't think it was that funny. We got detention after school for two weeks. We saw Ricky and Gary there. Ricky and Gary got detention because they were caught cheating on a test. When Ricky got home, his father beat his ass. I wasn't allowed to talk to anyone for two weeks. I was grounded and was not allowed out of the house either. Gary was not allowed to leave the house or talk to anyone. Rich Barton got fed cookies and ice cream. Rich Barton could do no wrong in his mom's eyes. All of us were best friends. we didn't allow anybody else to be part of our group. We trusted one another, and we helped one another. We spoke with one another, and that was all we needed from one another when we were upset or if we cried. We didn't look at them like they were weak; we took them under our wing to help them. That was our family. This is why the story is hard to write.

We were together from elementary school. I told my friends Ricky Kasso, Gary Lauwers, and Mark Florimonte I was trying out for the wrestling team.

Ricky and Gary said, "Albert, that sounds like a good idea. You got a lot of anger. You need to release it one way or another."

I was good at every sport that I played. It was like releasing a lion within a pack of sheep; I won every time. I signed up for the wrestling team and practiced with a bunch of guys, and the coach was named Thomas.

After one day of practice, Coach Thomas said, "Albert, you are a natural. Albert, you were born to do this sport. I've never had a kid at your age with so much skill and talent as you, Albert. I hope you stick with it, son. You can go places with this, Albert. I'll see you at practice tomorrow."

I thought Coach Thomas was just blowing smoke up my ass, but I went along with it. I said, "Thank you, sir. I'll be there tomorrow after class."

After practice, I went home and called up Rich Barton. I said, "What are you doing?"

Rich Barton said that Mark, Gary, and Ricky Kasso "Are hang out at his house, smoking weed. Do you want to come over, Albert?"

I said, "Yeah, my mom is making dinner, so after I'm done eating, I'll come over. And we'll burn up together. It should be about twenty minutes."

Richy replied, "Okay, sounds good."

Then I hung up the phone, and my mother made dinner—chicken a mash, potatoes, and gravy. While we were having dinner, I told my mother that I was going over to Rich's house to hang out for a little bit.

Mom said, "Okay. If you have homework, make sure you finish it."

I said, "Yeah, whatever," then walked over to Rich Barton's house and knocked on the door.

Richie's mom, Sally Barton, opened the door.

I asked, "Is Richie here?"

His mother replied, "Yeah, he's downstairs. Tell him to lower the radio. His father is trying to rest, and it's getting late. You guys have school in the morning."

Ricky Kasso, Gary, Mark, Richy Barton, and I sat in his room, smoking weed. We put the purple light on, we were listening to Black Sabbath, vegging out, and bullshitting about girls in school. As you can see, we were very close—much closer than people realize.

As the school year went on, I became a good athlete. I was a beast when it came to sports. The captain of the wrestling team, Rob Binary, could not make it to the meet, and the coach put me in a higher weight class because Coach Thomas was short one man and felt that I could handle it. The guy was much bigger than me, and he intimidated me. He weighed twenty pounds more than me and was six-foot-one, and I was five-foot-nine.

The word had traveled fast; the whole school came to see me wrestle because I was very strong and fast. The guy was from Massapequa. His name was Jay. He was the captain of his team in Massapequa. We both got called out to the mat. Each round was three minutes. When the bell rang, we went for it. Everybody in the gym stopped in their tracks and clapped their hands. It sounded like thunder cheering for me to win. The guy was much heavier; he was weighing me down, and I didn't know how to count o'clock him. I got angry, grabbed his knee, twisted it, dislocated it, and broke the tibia bone. Then I got on top and pinned him. The whole school was surprised that I was that strong and fast and that I hurt most of the people who got on the mat to wrestle against me. My reputation intimidated people and made them hesitant to go against me. I finally realized that the more angry I became, the better I became in sports. I was taking my anger out and putting it on the field, and I was unstoppable. Everybody came to the school and tournaments just to watch me hurt people on the field or in the matches.

By the end of eighth grade, I had scouts looking at me. I was a hot item. There were times I wanted to leave sports, but Coach Thomas would follow me around and would not let me go. He had big plans for me, and he wanted me to go to the Olympics.

Everybody had big plans for me, but that wasn't what I wanted in my life. I wanted one thing. I wanted my mother to care about me, and I couldn't understand why I felt so neglected, why Mom didn't care for me the way I wanted her to.

NINTH GRADE

In my final year in Northport Junior High, Ricky Kasso's stepfather was the coach of the football team and the gym teacher. Ricky Kasso was on the football team along with Robert Atkinson.

As the year went on, Ricky Kasso was forced to play football. Robert Atkinson was the quarterback and the captain of the football team. Robert called all the plays. Ricky Kasso and Robert became good friends.

Robert Atkinson thought Ricky Kasso was goofy and funny. Ricky is very shy but a good person One day, Ricky Kasso told his stepfather he didn't want to play football anymore, and Ricky's stepfather flipped out on him. And when he quit the football team, his stepfather got mad and kicked him out of the house.

Ricky Kasso came over to my house, upset, and said, "Albert, my father kicked me out of the house."

I spoke to Mom and told Mom that Ricky was kicked out of his house. And my mother wanted to know why he got kicked out. It was because Ricky Kasso did not want to play football anymore. My mother was disgusted at Ricky's stepfather.

Ricky Kasso started to cry. I could see the tears going down his face, and my mom hugged him. I never told anyone about that day till now. My mother said to Ricky, "You can stay with us, Ricky. It's okay. We love you. You'll be okay. And Ricky, if you stay with us, you have to go to school no matter what, okay?"

Ricky replied, "Yes, Mrs. Q" (that was her name to everyone back then), and Ricky agreed to it. So Ricky Kasso stayed with us.

I was on the soccer and the wrestling teams and studying, so my time was full of activities.

Gary had fallen in love with my sister Debbie. Ricky Kasso fell in love with Sarah Gotti, who lived around the corner from me. Mark Florimonte fell in love with my sister Wendy, and I fell in love with a girl named Sharon from Kings Park. So the only person who did not have a girlfriend was Richie Barton.

*****

Ninth grade was finally over, and it was summertime. Everyone had girlfriends, and everyone was happy and had a great summer. And then we were ready for school. Ricky was also back home. Everyone was happy he didn't have to play football anymore.

I was close to being done with school—two more years left after tenth grade.

I was happy that lots of scouts came to look at me because of my wrestling and soccer abilities. I knew for sure I was going to get scholarships, and who knows? Coach Thomas kept pushing me for the Olympics. So far, everything was looking great for me.

Ricky was happy because he didn't have to be on the football team in Northport Junior High with his stepfather. It was a new start for Ricky Kasso.

Gary and Debbie Quinones were in love.

I was in love with Sharon Johnson from Kings Park.

Ricky Kasso was in love with Sarah Goti from Northport.

Mark Florimonte and Wendy Quinones were in love.

We had a friendship after all these years from elementary school, so there was a confident feeling when going into the tenth grade. We were happy we were all together and still had friends.

These guys and my family are in my heart to this day.

TENTH GRADE

Now it was the beginning of tenth grade. School had just started. It was our first day going to school. Northport High School was a little far for us to walk, so we had to wait at the bus stop down the road on the corner of Maple Avenue and Main Street at 7:00 AM.

The bus picked up Rich Barton and me on the corner of Maple Avenue and Main Street.

The bus made its rounds, picking up the rest of the kids. We got to school at Northport High School.

The bus arrived at Northport High School at around 7:30 AM, and we hung out in the common areas where everyone hung out in groups in front of the school. We were waiting for the bell to ring for us to go to class.

Ricky Kasso, Gary Lauwers, Mark Florimonte, Rich Barton, and I had coffee and rolled up a blunt to smoke before class.

EYEWITNESS

Like usual, every year, we did the same. I was selling weed at the time, and everyone knew that if you wanted to smoke weed, you had to come to me. My next-door neighbor was a biker and Debbie Jager's boyfriend; he was the leader of the Pagans (that was a motorcycle gang).

The head pagans Tom drove over in a van. In the back of the van, he would have hefty bags full of weed—all different types of weed and hundred pounds of weed. It was quick, easy cash, and I knew all the potheads because I was one of them and a jock.

Back then, everyone was smoking pot. It was like having a cigarette. It was all about sex, drugs, and rock and roll.

There was a concert every weekend. And hanging out in Northport Park, Ricky played the guitar. He was pretty good at it. Gary would sing whatever Ricky played. Gary seemed to know every song and these stories that nobody knew. The group I was in was small, and we stuck together. Gary would sing Led Zeppelin or The Doors. Ricky Kasso and Gary Lauwers were very close friends, and not a lot of people realize that. And I'm trying to let everyone know the truth about who these people really are.

The following day, I went back to school at lunchtime. Randy had come to me in school. Randy Guther approached me and said he had something he wanted to show me in a brown paper bag. Randy Guther and I went into the handicap elevator, and I said, "What is it you want to show me, Randy?"

Randy Guther

Indian Graveyard

Randy said to me that he and his friend went to the graveyard, and he dug up the grave and took the hand and the skull and put it in a brown paper bag to Northport High School to show me.

I yelled at Randy and said that was somebody's family member. "Have you lost your goddamn mind?

Why are you showing me this, Randy? Who else have you been showing it to?"

Randy said he showed Lori Walsh.

"That's real smart, Randy," I replied. "Do you know that Lori Walsh's dad is a detective in the Northport police office? Randy, don't get me wrapped up in this shit. Stay the hell away from me. That was the stupidest thing you could've ever done, Randy."

Randy Guther replied, "He wanted to see if there was any jewelry in there."

"Why did you keep the hand and head, Randy? Keep it away from me and keep away from me. You're out of your mind, Randy Guther." Then I proceeded to open the elevator and walked away from Randy.

Randy was standing in the elevator, scared to death that Lori Walsh was going to tell her dad, who was a police officer.

On the following day, I was sitting at home, watching TV, when I saw that Randy was arrested for digging up the Indian graveyard. Rumor has it that Laurie Walsh told her father. Randy was arrested and put *on probation. Randy was all over the news. The news started saying it was a cult, and the media frenzy began.*

Huntington graffiti in Northport Park

Shortly after that, people from the next town over—Huntington—came down to Northport Park, writing stuff all over our parks and all over the town. We were pissed off at Huntington football team for writing that stuff—like Satan devil worshipers stuff—all over our town and parks and our building. Everybody in Northport was pissed off at that time.

A few months went by, and things started to calm down in Northport. It was a crazy time back then; a bunch of us were pissed off at Huntington because of what they did to our town—writing crap in our parks and all over our town. Now there was a vendetta; to get back at Huntington, rumor has it that a bunch of kids went up to Huntington and started writing shit on their schools and in their town. It slowly became a war between the Huntington High School and Northport High School. Huntington came to Northport with a group of kids and supposedly jumped some kids in Northport. Then we set up an arrangement to have a big brawl in East Northport's park with Huntington.

Huntington accepted the challenge.

Ricky Kasso

ALBERT QUINONES

Gary Lauwers

Mark Florimonte

Albert Quinones 1984

A week later, I was at Rich Barton's house with Ricky Kasso, Gary Lauwers, and Mark Florimonte. I was getting ready for the fight. We had our leather jackets and motorcycle boots on, and each of us had pool sticks, and we were all ready to open a can of whoop-ass on Huntington High School.

It was around 9:00 p.m., and it was a crystal-clear night out. The Huntington football team came up to the East Northport Park. Huntington had fifty people from the school waiting for us in the East Northport Park to show up. The plan was for Huntington to get to the park and sit in the middle of the park, then Northport High School would show up and circle around Huntington High School with two hundred people from Northport. The people from Northport would strong-arm Huntington High School and beat their asses. The Northport police had no idea what was going on. Northport people showed up in their cars and circled the park with the cars and left the headlights on to keep the park lit up. About two hundred people from Northport got out of their cars, ran into the park, and started whipping Huntington's ass. There were bats, chain, and pool stick, whatever anyone could get their hands on, and Huntington High School, they were getting their asses beaten for what they did to the Northport Village school and park—for the graffiti in our ground. Across the street from the park was the fire department from East Northport. The sirens went off, and the police started rushing into the park. They finally realized that there was a brawl going on. People were getting hit with chains, bats, sticks, bottles, whatever anyone got their hands, and everyone who was from Northport started running out of the park to their cars. The Huntington football team got their ass beaten really bad, and people were arrested. There was an ambulance to take the people from Huntington to the hospital.

That was a day no one would forget. It was a sad but proud day. It showed that everyone stuck together.

We all met back at Rich Barton's house. Ricky Kasso, Gary Lauwers, and I went down into Richie's basement, where his room was. We got pretty banged up. We put the music on. Rich was saying how he got hit in the ribs with a chain, and I got hit in the ribs with nightstick. We started laughing, but it was hard for us to breathe. So we told Gary to go into Rich's closet, break out the bong, and put on the purple light. We started smoking weed, and we put the music on. We were laughing our asses off, but we were also all in pain. Shortly after that, Rich's mom screamed down the stairs, telling us it was time for us to go home. Richie didn't argue with his mom on that; we all agreed on it because we were in pain. So we went home to try to relax. Oh, that was the night Gary stole Ricky Kasso's one hundred tabs of LSD—a hundred hits and his money—out of Ricky's coat pocket. This was not the first time Gary Lauwer stole from Ricky.

So Ricky went up to his girlfriend, Sarah. I went back to my house, and Gary went back to his house.

Richie stayed home. Ricky called up Gary and asked him if he saw his money and acid. Gary said no.

Ricky called me and asked if I saw his acid and money. I said no. Then Ricky Kasso called up Richie and asked him if he left his money and acid at his house. Richie said no too. Ricky Kasso asked Richie Barton to look around to see if he could find the acid and money and to please call him back. Later on, when he called Ricky and said that no, it was not there, Ricky said it had to be there. This was not the first time Gary had robed Ricky Kasso, but it might be the last time. On the following day, rumor has it that Gary Lauwers was selling acid, and the acid was Ricky Kasso's one hundred hits of acid at $20 a head, which was $2000 and worth of work stolen from Ricky's pocket; and the worst thing is that it was his best friend that stole from him; he stole enough to get him back on his feet and get him a place to live to get away from his stepfather.

Word got back to Ricky, and Ricky was pissed. At lunchtime, Ricky and Gary were having a big argument. Gary had taken Ricky's LSD. No one wanted to buy the acid in the town because it was

Ricky's Gary was selling. Gary had a hard time selling it in Northport.

Ricky Kasso was so pissed off at that moment and hurt that his friend would do that to him. Ricky did not put his hands on Gary because he didn't know what to do. Ricky walked away, hurt and pissed off.

I heard what happened and wanted to talk to Gary. I asked, "Is it true you stole Ricky's money and his drugs?"

Gary said, "Yeah, I don't know why I did it. I was high. I don't know why. I'm sorry. I'm gonna pay Ricky back."

I said to Gary, "You have to stop stealing from people."

Gary said, "My parents cut me off. I have no money, and I don't know what to do."

"Gary, get a job. That's what you need to do, but you need to straighten this out with Ricky Kasso. And Gary, you need to pay him. I'm not gonna have this shit go on between all of us, especially in my house because you're going out with my sister Debbie, and don't ever think about stealing from me because I will whip your ass."

"Albert, I would never do that to you."

"I don't know anymore. You just did it to Ricky. I'm letting you know, Gary, you need to straighten this out with Ricky. ASAP, bro, okay? I don't want to be in the middle. This is between you two. Now fix it, Gary."

"Okay, Albert, I will. I promise."

Then I walked away.

I had wrestling practice and did not make it. Coach Thomas was pissed off at me. He heard what happened with the fight up in East Northport. Coach Thomas said to me, "Albert, you need to stay out of trouble. You have a lot of good things going for you in your future. Albert, you're going to screw it up if you keep screwing around with these people. You could possibly make it to the Olympics if you keep your grades up and stay out of trouble. You do have a very good shot at it."

I replied, "Okay, Coach Thomas."

A few weeks went by. Gary still did not pay Ricky.

Ricky Kasso was fighting with his parents because his grades were down and he was always smoking pot. His parents were mad. They decided to place him in South Oaks for rehab.

Ricky Kasso's mother and stepfather drove Ricky to South Oaks the following day for rehab.

Ricky had gone into rehab, but Ricky called me up and said that his friends were going to break him out.

I started to laugh. "Good luck. They have you deep in the boondocks in the woods." I didn't believe his story.

Ricky said to me, "This place sucks, and I'm just a kid. I'm not wasting any time in here. I'm coming home by tomorrow."

I thought he was playing. I replied, "I have a bag of weed if you want to smoke some," which instilled laughing The following night Ricky had a couple friends drive up to South Oaks rehab and Ricky snuck out the window late at night, went through the woods and down the road, and hopped into his friend's car. South Oaks notified Ricky's mother and stepfather that Ricky had escaped from South Oaks. Ricky had no idea that South Oaks told his family that. Ricky Kasso was on the run and he came to Rich Barton's house when we all met up and were partying. Ricky decided he was going to go home, sneak into the house, steal some clothes, and come back out. When Ricky got to his house, his stepfather beat Ricky Kasso's ass and told him never to come back to the house and to get his ass back to rehab; otherwise, he was never coming back home. Ricky came to me and told me what his father did. I said, "What did you expect, Ricky?" and told him I would speak to my mother to see if he could stay with us.

I told my mom that Ricky got thrown out again. Mom asked, "What for now?"

I said, "They just don't get along. Can Ricky stay here for a little bit, Mom?"

Mom said, "Okay, he can stay here, but Ricky has to go to school. And you guys cannot be up all night, smoking pot." Mom told Ricky Kasso that if he can't follow those simple rules, he would have to leave. They called my mom Mrs. Q.

She was the town mom, and everybody loved her except me. I had my reasons for not liking my mom.

Gary found out Ricky was out. Gary kept his distance

Gary didn't come over to my place as much. I didn't think much about it, and Ricky didn't say anything about Gary owing him money as if it was forgotten about.

Ricky mentioned that he met a guy named Jimmy Troiano upstate in rehab, but the guy was always in trouble with the law for drugs and robbery. But he seemed okay.

I told Ricky, "Anyone that's robbing people is not okay, and you need to stay the hell away from him."

Ricky told me Jimmy's parents were thinking about moving to Northport and said that Jimmy was adopted. Jimmy didn't have anyone, and his father beat him up just like Ricky's father beat him up.

I said to Ricky, "Well, Ricky, I hope Jimmy doesn't move here. I don't want anything to do with Jimmy." After I said that to Ricky, the discussion about Jimmy was over.

*****

Tenth grade was finally coming to an end. We had a couple of weeks of school left, then the parties in the summer would go on nonstop. There would be sex, drugs, and rock and roll.

THE SUMMER OF 1984

Ricky Kasso and I went over to Rich Barton's house to hang out with Richy Barton and Mark Florimonte.

As we were sitting around, smoking weed and listening to music. I suggested that we should go to the Northport VA water tower and hang out on top of the water tower and smoke some weed and put some graffiti on it. Everyone thought it was a good idea, and we wanted to do something crazy and fun. As we cut a hole through the fence to the VA hospital water towers, we started climbing up the water tower because we were stoned, laughing, and thinking it was funny. We got to the top of the water tower and were dipping our feet in the water, laughing like adolescent children, and we started pissing in the water tower, laughing about everyone in the town drinking our piss. As time went on, we decided to leave. We then climbed down the water tower stoned out of my face from smoking weed. We all went home and followed day a bunch of kids heard what we did. Some other kids wanted to go up there themselves to make graffiti art. Then we decided not to follow them. They got up to the top of the tower and started to make graffiti art, putting their names on it with cans of spray paint up. The sirens went off. The cops circled around the VA water tower. Helicopters with spotlights were over the tower, and their lights on everyone that climbed up it. They were forced to come down from the tower. They were all arrested, and the parents had to repaint the tower that they graffitied on. These are some of the things we did as kids as a group. That's how close we were as kids.

School was coming close to the end. Ricky had just passed by the skin of his teeth. I had an 85 average. I wanted to keep those grades because I loved being on the wrestling team.

Gary slowly started hanging out with Billy Leason from Harborfields High School when he found out that Ricky was out of rehab. I guess that in a way, he was scared because Gary still did not pay Ricky back for the drugs and money he stole.

The following day, it was a beautiful day out. Mark and Richie Barton came over to my house, and then we went up to Northport Junior High, where we hung out on the side of the Ground Round restaurant and smoked weed. And that was where everyone would hang out.

Jimmy Troiano started walking across to the Northport Junior High School field. He introduced himself to me, and Ricky said, "Albert, that's the guy

I was going to rehab with." Right off the bat, I didn't like Jimmy, and Jimmy felt the vibe.

Jimmy Troiano tried to buy some weed from me, but I wouldn't sell it to Jimmy. Jimmy the street thug. He knew that I did not like him, and I knew that he and I were gonna have problems.

Jimmy and I looked at each other, both with a dislike for the other.

Jimmy look at Ricky and told Ricky he was leaving and "I'll call you later, Ricky." Jimmy started walking away.

I look at Ricky and said, "I told you I didn't want him around us, or our crew."

Ricky Kasso was quiet, and no one knew what to say.

"Ricky, you told me how Jimmy robbed houses, stole cars, robbed stores, and beat people up. I don't want Jimmy around us. If you want to hang out with Jimmy, then take your shit and get out of my house."

Ricky Kasso replied to me, saying he understood and would stay away from Jimmy.

A couple of weeks went by when the rumors started flying around town that Jimmy Troiano had robbed the Midway—a small smoke shop in Northport

Village. Jimmy Troiano stole many things like paraphernalia pipes, T-shirts, knives, bandannas, leather wallets, and many other things. Ziggy, the owner of the smoke shop, was a very dear close friend of ours. This made things more complicated. It made everybody angry.

Within two weeks, another house behind my house on 85 Maple Ave. was robbed. Rumor has it that Jimmy robbed that house as well.

Rumor has it that Jimmy robbed Randy Guther's house as well. Within two weeks of being in Northport Village, Jimmy Troiano started the crime wave of stealing and took it to another level.

No one wanted Jimmy around.

Richy Barton, Mark Florimonte, Ricky Kasso, and Gary came over to my house with their girlfriends and mine. We were having a barbecue in the backyard. I was making hamburgers for Mark, Richie, and everybody else. Mark said that Sandrine was having a surprise birthday party for Chuck, her boyfriend, that night. It was all still up in the air; it all depended on if she could get the kegs of beer for the party from the beer distributor.

It was very hot outside. That day, I made a suggestion that we should all walk down to the beach, hang out at the beach, and play Frisbee. Everyone agreed and thought it was a great idea. We finished eating. We had the volleyball, the net, and the Frisbees, and we started walking up to the beach. Richy Barton had the big radio boom box and put a tape in and started playing hard rock and roll, and we were all in our bathing suits.

As we got to the beach, and we set up everything on the beach. The girls were lying down on the blankets in their bathing suits. We set up the volleyball net then started playing hard rock 'n' roll Led Zeppelin, and we had the music blasting hard rock and roll. It was a great day to be at the beach.

The sun started going down. We decided to go home and get ready to go out to Northport Village and hang out. We started to leave the beach and walk back home.

Ricky mentioned that Karen Novollino was going out with Jimmy Troiano. I didn't really hang out with Karen that much, so I didn't know much about Karan. I said to Ricky Kasso, "As long as Jimmy stays away from my sisters Debbie and Wendy, I don't care what Jimmy does." We got back to my house, and we started smoking some weed. And the girls were getting ready to go to Northport Park.

EYEWITNESS

Rich Barton, Marks Florimonte, Gary Lauwers, and I decided to go ahead to Northport Park and have the girls meet up with us after they were done getting dressed. Shortly after that, Debbie, Wendy, and Sarah met all of us at the gazebo in the park. Rumor has it that Sandrin was having a party for her boyfriend, Chuck Cheshire. She was able to pick up two kegs of beer and ordered three–to six-foot-long hero sandwiches, potato salad, macaroni salad, and all the works for her boyfriend Chuck's birthday. Everybody started heading to Chuck's girlfriend's house for the party, and as we approached the front door, Sandrine called me over to the side and said that Ricky, Jimmy, and Gary were not allowed at the party and that she didn't want those guys in her house because they would ruin the surprise party for her boyfriend. I replied that I understood but that I could not leave my friends behind. Jimmy had an attitude and was going to go to the party anyway.

I said, "No, that wouldn't be right. We're not gonna do that." I told Debbie, Wendy, Sarah, and Karen to enjoy the party. "We will find something else to do. We will meet up would you guys tomorrow, so just have a good time." I then said to Jimmy,

Ricky, and Gary, "What did you expect with the reputation you guys have? I don't blame them. I wouldn't want you guys at my party either. I started laughing at them. Now I'm stuck with you guys, so let's make the best of it."

Ricky had picked up another sheet of acid that had one hundred tabs. Jimmy suggested we should do some acid, so we all agreed, and it sounded like a good idea. We took a hit each, and Ricky took two hits of LSD.

The trail to Aztakea woods

EYEWITNESS

The map leading to the crime scene from Northport Park

Northport Aztakea Woods Crime Scene

It was about 9:30 PM, and it was damp and wet outside. So we took a hit each. Then Ricky, Gary, Jimmy, and I started walking up Main Street.

Then I suggested to everybody that we should go to Dunkin' Donuts.

"Because I have a friend that works there. We can get some free food from him at Dunkin Donuts," Jimmy said.

Everyone agreed that it was a good idea to go to Dunkin' Donuts. Jimmy suggested that we all go to Aztakea Woods to trip out. Everyone agreed that it was a good idea.

"Let's trip out at Aztakea Woods," Gary said. It sounded like a good idea too.

Jimmy said he had been there with Ricky and that it looked like a good place to hang out. We agreed, and as we were walking, it started to rain. But we kept on walking up Main Street going east then made a right going up Laurel Avenue southbound to Dunkin' Donuts. Jimmy and Ricky were walking behind me and Gary, about ten to fifteen feet, and I didn't like that; it was annoying me.

Gary said, "Is everything all right, Albert? Is Ricky still mad at me?"

I said, "For what?"

Gary said, "I didn't pay Ricky back yet. I just haven't had any money."

I said, "Well, you still need to pay Ricky Kasso back. I haven't heard anything about it, so I'm sure it's all right."

I turned back and said to Ricky and Jimmy, "Why are you guys walking so far behind us?" I then came up with sarcastic remark and said to Ricky and Jimmy, "If you lovebirds want to be alone, then feel free to go your own way, and then we'll go our own way. And if you're going to hang out with us, then all of us need to hang out together."

Jimmy did not like the remark that I made. I felt bad vibes coming from Jimmy, the tension was in the air. Jimmy didn't respond back to me. Jimmy was not about to give up. He was going to get back at Albert and every one. Jimmy had a plan devised. No one knew what was about to happen; everyone's lives were going to change dramatically.

This was the second time I had done acid. Ricky Kasso was acting weird. I asked Ricky Kasso what was wrong.

Jimmy was bragging about how Ricky did five more hits of acid.

I said, "Are you kidding me, Ricky?"

Ricky said, "Yeah."

I said, "Why did you do five more hits, Ricky? You've never done that many before."

It was around eleven-thirty at night. Ricky Kasso replied, "I don't know why. I just did it."

I said to Jimmy, "Did you talk Ricky into doing five more hits of LSD?"

Jimmy didn't say anything. I could see Ricky was starting to trip out.

Jimmy said to me, "I'm not his mommy. Ricky is a grown man, and Ricky can do what he wants."

Now the tension was bigger than ever between Jimmy and I.

It was about 12:30 AM when we made it to Dunkin' Donuts and got some food. Then started heading west on 25-A Street. We were tripping out at this point and really didn't feel like eating any more food. I was worrying about Ricky, and Gary was too. But Gary did not say anything to Ricky. Gary did not upset Ricky. He owed Ricky money still. We started walking to Aztakea Woods. We made a right going north on Church Street then made a left, going west on Franklin Street.

We started walking down the street to the trail that led us to the Northport Aztakea Woods. Jimmy was leading the way, and we started walking down the path in the woods. It was very dark, and the ground was wet from when it was drizzling before for a short time.

We got to the center of the woods where it was cleared out; it was where we used to hang out and have fires. As we went deeper into the woods, we passed the campground. There was a cleared-out lot of rolling green grass for about a half an acre that was very well maintained and pruned. It was where kids used to lay out blankets, stare at the stars, and listen to music. Gary and I decided to get some wood to start a fire because it was very damp out and wet. It was very clear that night, but for some reason, it just didn't feel peaceful in the air. I didn't know if it was Jimmy's energy. Jimmy and Ricky were just standing there while Gary and I were looking for wood and twigs to start a fire. Gary and I got all the wood together. We made a tepee with the wood and had a hard time trying to start a fire since the wood was too wet.

Gary said, "Listen, my Levi's jacket is too short anyway. How about I cut off the sleeves to my jacket?"

At this point, I was pissed and said, "Do whatever you want."

Ricky said, "No, that sounds like a good idea. Gary, take off your jacket and use the sleeves."

I was shocked that Ricky said anything to Gary. It was the first time he spoke a word to Gary through the whole night.

Ricky handed a knife to Gary, and Gary cut the sleeves off his jacket and placed the sleeves in the teepee of wood to start the fire.

I saw Ricky with a knife, and I question Ricky. "Where did you get the knife from?"

Ricky replied that he got it from Jimmy, who got it from the Midway when he robbed it two weeks ago.

Jimmy had a smirk on his face and kind of chuckled and laughed under his breath.

Jimmy and I were butting heads throughout the course of the night.

Now it was around 2:00 AM. I didn't push the issue of the knife with Ricky because I didn't want Ricky to think that I was being his daddy, or making

Ricky Kasso look like a baby. We got the fire started, and it was a big bonfire. It lit up the whole area. Any dampness in the air, the fire took it all away. Jimmy started playing some music. I think he played either Iron Maiden or the song "War Pigs" at the time. I'm not very sure.

Everything seemed to calm down a little bit. The tension in the air started lifting. We were listening to music. Ricky and Jimmy were on one side of the fire, and Gary and I were on the other side of the fire. It looked like two teams. They were on one team while Gary and I were on another team.

Ricky was not acting like himself. He said to Gary, "You have my money."

Gary said, "No, I don't have it, but I'll get it for you tomorrow, Ricky."

Ricky replied to Gary, "You've had over two months to get my money. What are you trying to do, make me look like a pussy in front of the whole town? Gary, you robbed me when you and I was fighting against Huntington side by side. It wasn't the first time, Gary. You robbed me again, Gary."

I didn't know what to say at that time. Ricky was 100 percent right. I had to back off and let them handle it like men. I was friends with Ricky, and I was friends with Gary.

Gary replied, "You're right, Rick." Gary said it out loud to Ricky, then Ricky called Gary out for a fight.

"If I fight you, Ricky, promise that it will be just be between you and me."

Ricky replied out loud, "Yes, but you're not gonna win, Gary, no matter what." (In a fight, whoever wins or loses, the debt will be forgiven, and all will start off on a clean slate.)

Ricky and Gary started walking toward each other. The fight was on. Ricky and Gary threw a punch at the same time, and they both landed the punch at the same time. Ricky and Gary stumbled back, and Ricky tripped over a log and fell on the ground. Gary shook his head, ran after Ricky, and got on top of Ricky. Then he started punching Ricky. Gary was winning, and Ricky could not break free of Gary. The fight looked like it was coming to an end, and it looked like Gary was going to win. I was getting ready to walk over and break up the fight. As I walked over to do so, Jimmy had run over to Gary and kicked Gary in the stomach, causing Gary to fall off of Ricky Kasso.

I ran over to Jimmy, shoved him against a tree, and said, "If you put your hands on Gary one more time or any of them, I will kill you, Jimmy."

Jimmy said, "Well, that's your boy, Ricky. He's losing."

I replied, "That's not how we do it in Northport. Maybe you pull that shit in jail and gang up on people, but we don't do that shit here, Jimmy."

I turned around and said to Gary, "Are you okay?"

Gary said, "I'm fine."

Albert said, "Do you still want to fight Ricky?"

Gary replied, "Only if Ricky still wants to fight."

Ricky was embarrassed, angry, and tripping out on acid. He was at his peak now. He felt belittled and disrespected and angry as hell now. We could see the anger and rage in his eyes now as he was tripping out on acid. Ricky said, "I am going to kill you! I'm not stopping until you're dead!" Ricky ran to Gary and grabbed Gary around the neck from behind. Then Ricky pulled a knife out and stabbed Gary once in the back.

I was in shock.

Jimmy said, "You started this! Now, Ricky, you have to finish it off!"

EYEWITNESS

I shouted at Jimmy and said, "What the hell are you talking about?"

Gary said, "Ricky, I promise you I'll pay you tomorrow. Just let me go, please."

I yelled at Ricky, "Put down the goddamn knife!" as I walked over to Ricky to try to calm him down and get the knife away from him.

Ricky Kasso swung his knife at me and almost cut me in the neck. As I approached Ricky again, Gary broke free from Ricky and started to run away. Ricky started running after Gary, and as Gary ran by Jimmy Troiano, Jimmy stuck his foot out to trip Gary causing him to fall to the ground as Gary was getting up. Ricky ran towards Gary and grabbed him around the neck and stabbed him two more times in the back. I went back to take the knife from Ricky, and Ricky swung. The knife at me again. I stepped back in shock, not believing that Ricky had the guts as well as the nerve to do that to me. I was trying to defuse the situation and calm him down. He was so far out of his mind. And I was scared for Gary and me. I saw the anger in Ricky's eyes again, and he was about to lose or give up that knife. If anyone got in his way, he was going to kill them. Ricky was out of his mind on acid.

Gary said, "Albert, he's going to kill me."

I said, "Gary, he's not gonna kill you. Ricky, put down the knife now."

Gary said to Albert, "Make sure you tell my mother I love her."

Ricky said, "Gary can go meet his maker and go to hell." Ricky then started stabbing Gary in back and stabbing Gary in the chest, working his way up to his neck.

I lost count of how many times Ricky stabbed Gary. Ricky stabbed Gary in the neck and hit a jugular vein, and the blood sprayed into my face and eyes. When I wiped the blood from my eyes, I saw that Gary was lying down on his back, and Ricky was standing above Gary with his knife in his hands. All of us were in shock. Gary's body starting moving because of muscle spasms, and Ricky jumped on top of Gary and started stabbing him his chest and eyes out so many times that I lost count.

I couldn't believe it was for real. I thought it was just a bad dream. I said to Ricky, "What did you just do? You just killed our best friend over what? Stupid drugs and some money!"

Ricky then didn't say anything.

Jimmy said, "Ricky, you can't just leave the body here."

Ricky was in shock.

Jimmy said to me, "If you say anything, you'll be the next one."

At this point, I did not know what to say. But okay, I am not telling anyone. I was devastated; my best friend just killed another one of my best friends. Who is the real animal in this picture? Was it Jimmy, who took advantage of Ricky Kasso's friendship, talked him into doing five more hits of acid, and planted seeds in Ricky's head, causing Ricky to flip out on his best friend? Or was Ricky Kasso, who carried out the act of crime on his best friend? Ricky grabbed Gary's arms while Jimmy grabbed Gary's legs, and they both carried Gary's body from the campfire deeper into the woods and covered the body with some more leaves and sticks. I stood there in shock, but I knew I had to get out of the woods, or I might be the next one lying down next to Gary. I had to play it real cool. Jimmy had control over Ricky's mind.

I stayed by the campfire, and I was covered in blood and was in shock, saying that this was just a bad dream and that this was not really happening. I had to stay cool, and the less said the better off things would be. I didn't want to give them any idea or make them think that I was going to say the wrong thing and have them kill me.

It was around five-thirty in the morning. I knew I had to get out of the woods. I knew they had to clean up, and they had nowhere else to go. I told them they needed to get to my house before my mother came home from work. I think that was the only reason why they let me live, and I couldn't let her see me covered in blood like that. As we were walking home, I was coming down from the acid trip. I keep saying in my head that this was not happening. I just saw my best friend get murdered by my other best friend, I was having a hard time processing that and my enemy, Jimmy Troiano, was praising Ricky for doing what he did to Gary, commending it as if didn't bother Jimmy. I was pissed off at Ricky for what he did inside. I know Jimmy had something to do with it. I needed to get everyone out of the woods. I was in shock and could not believe my ears when I heard what Jimmy Troiano said to Ricky Kasso that night. At this point, I did not know who Ricky was anymore that night. I just wanted to get away from those two before anything happened to me. The sun was coming up and you could hear the birds chirping. As we were walking to my house, I noticed my mother's car wasn't in the driveway.

It was around six-fifteen now, and my mother would be home at around seven-thirty. I was pressed for time too. It was bad enough that I lost a friend. Now I had to get everyone in and out of the house before my mother gets home.

I said to Jimmy and Ricky Kasso, "You guys have ten minutes each to shower, get your clothes off, and put them in a brown paper bag. When you guys are done taking a shower, I will give you guys new clothes to wear."

It was around 6:45 AM when Jimmy and Ricky finished taking a shower and changing. I told Jimmy and Ricky to take their clothes and that they had to leave because my mother was coming home at about 7:15 or 7:30 AM, and no one was allowed in the house when she wasn't home. Jimmy looked at me and had an attitude; it was as if my house belonged to him. With an arrogant jailhouse mentality, Jimmy and Ricky took their clothes that were in brown paper bags and proceeded to walk out the front door while I was still covered in blood. My mother would be home in fifteen minutes. I had to really speed it up; I had to get in and out of the shower and clean everything up before my mom came home from work. I was still in shock, trying to make sense of what happened while I was showering, washing the blood off my face and body. I was relieved that Jimmy and Ricky had left and didn't turn on me in the woods. I got out of the shower, put my clothes in a brown bag, and put on blue sweatpants, a T-shirt, and socks on. My mother pulled up in the driveway and came into the house. I walked into my bedroom, shut the door, locked it.

My mother yelled upstairs and asked if I was awake. I said yes.

My mother then said, "I saw Jimmy and Ricky walking down the road. What is Ricky doing with Jimmy? And I hope Jimmy wasn't in the house because you know I don't want him in my house."

I replied, "Ricky is not staying here. I don't know what he's doing with Jimmy, and I really don't care. And Jimmy was not here." Then I shut the door, went to bed, and did not sleep for a week. I was still in shock that this happened.

EYEWITNESS

Rumor has it that Jimmy and Ricky Kasso stayed at Jimmy Troiano's house for a few days, and then their plan was to head upstate to Saratoga. Jimmy's parents had a place upstate. Jimmy was very familiar with the upstate area because Jimmy Troiano lived in Albany for most of his life. Rumor has it that after a few days, Jimmy took his father's handgun, went to Middleville Road in Northport, and stood in the middle of the road, pointing the gun at a car. The man in the car was coming home from work, and Jimmy and Ricky carjacked the car to go upstate to Saratoga to pick up more drugs, only to find out that the man that was coming home late from work was the DA from the court district of Suffolk County, Long Island.

*****

It had been over a week now, and I hadn't left the house or spoken to anyone. I was still trying to process what really happened.

My mother was at work, and Mark Florimonte and Rich Barton went over to my house to hang out with Wendy, Debbie, and me.

ALBERT QUINONES

Everybody was hanging out, smoking weed, doing cocaine, drinking. Mark and Richie called me off to the side and told me that they knew what Ricky did. I was in shock, wondering how they found out. Apparently, Jimmy had taken Mark, Richie, and a few people up to the woods where Gary was killed, showing people the body. I told Mark and Richie not to tell my sisters Debbie or Wendy; the less anyone knew the better. People in the town were starting to talk, and shortly after that, the cops came to my house, knocking on the door. I knew the cop from walking around Northport Village. The police officer had just gotten a call saying the house around the corner might be getting robbed, and his partner wasn't there, so he asked if I could back him up.

I knew that was bullshit, but I told the police officer that I would go with him anyway. I knew something was going down but didn't want my sisters Debbie and Wendy to know what was going on and have Debbie and Wendy worry about me. Then I walked out the door with the cop and got into the police officer's car. We drove down to the end of Maple Avenue then made a right. Just as we made the right, the blue-and-white police car pulled to the side, and three black undercover cars pulled up to the car. They pulled me out of the police officer car and put me in the black unmarked detective's car. With four detectives, there were two detectives in the front. I was in the center back seat with one detective on my left-hand side and one on my right-hand side—to make sure I did not escape.

They started driving me down Motor Parkway to the court building. Just then, he started asking me if I saw Gary and where Ricky and Jimmy were. I told him I hadn't seen Gary and that I didn't know where Ricky or Jimmy Troiano were.

The four detectives drove their car to the back of the court building around 9:30 PM. They took me out of the car and walked me through the back door of the building. We got into an elevator and got off on the second floor, and they walked me into a private room.

The detectives took me and sat me in a chair, and they began asking me questions about Ricky and Jimmy like where they were.

I replied that I didn't know where they were.

The detectives didn't wanna hear that, and they began to hit the back of my head, my stomach, and my ribs. They kept repeating the same question: "Where is Gary?" And every time I said I didn't know, they would hit me.

Every question they asked me, I refused to answer and would be hit. They had me, at one point, spread against the wall, my legs and arms spread apart, and kicked me in the balls many times. They made me do that routine a few times. They kept telling me they knew what happened and wanted to know where Ricky and Jimmy were while I honestly and really didn't know where they were. At one time, they used a telephone book and a police baton and put it across my ribs, and they would hit the telephone book with a nightstick, causing me to have bruised ribs and making it hard for me to breathe.

For over four and a half hours, I took a beating and still did not say a word, and they could not get any information from me. At this time, the police gave up; they said, "Maybe this guy doesn't know anything."

They drove me back to my house, handed me a police card, and said that if I heard of anything, to please give them a call. I looked at them in shock; I couldn't believe that they would have the nerve to even say that to me, but I was not in a position to create conflict.

They dropped me off at my house. I went inside. Everybody was asking why it took me so long to get back home. I had nothing to say about it. I called the guys outside and said, "Listen, I just got beat up for four and a half hours. This shit's going down." I asked Mark if he knew where Ricky Kasso and Jimmy were.

Mark replied, "Rumor has it that Jimmy went to his house upstate with Ricky to get some drugs."

I knew this shit was going down now, not knowing which way this ball was going to turn. I decided to stay away from my house as much as possible. I called up Rich Barton and Mark Florimonte to ask them to come over. I wanted to talk to them but not on the phone.

I had a feeling this shit was going to hit the fan either today or tomorrow. I asked Mark and Rich to stay with me later on in the evening.

They stayed over at my house because I was scared, and I said to the guys, "I think we should go down to the Northport docks because it's going to go down today. I had this feeling and ask Richie Barton to go get the fishing poles and buckets. I want to stay away from the house as much as possible. I had called my mother at work and told her that I was going to go fishing early in the morning at around five on the docks, and she said okay and told me to just to be safe and stay out of trouble.

I said, "Okay, Mom. I love you."

She said, "I love you too, Al."

Albert Quinones 1984

EYEWITNESS

Mark Florimonte

Northport Docks

Around 5:00 AM., we started heading down to the docks. Rich, Mark Florimonte, and I all had a bad feeling this was the day. Hell was going to break loose.

We made it to the Northport docks that had benches. On the docks, all three of us sat on the bench on the dock, set up the fishing poles, and started fishing.

Jimmy and Ricky had just driven back from Saratoga and had a whole bunch of drugs on them in the back of Jimmy's boom box radio; Jimmy had removed all the D batteries and packed it with drugs. Jimmy knew where to score all the drugs he wanted because Jimmy had lived in Albany, New York, so it was an easy score for Jimmy.

When Jimmy and Ricky got back to Northport at around 5:30 AM, they parked behind the Midway in Northport—the place that Jimmy had robbed a month before. Jimmy did not realize when he told Lori Walsh what Ricky did to Gary. Jimmy didn't realize that Lori Walsh's father was a police officer, and she told her father what Ricky did. And now everybody was looking for Jimmy Troiano and Ricky Kasso. Jimmy had called up Karen, his girlfriend, to tell her that it was over between them too and he and Ricky was moving to California, but Karen replied to

Jimmy, "Are you serious, Jimmy? Really?" Jimmy said yes, and then he hung up on Karen.

Karen then was very angry at Jimmy and was about to drop the biggest bomb on him, and he had no idea it was coming. Karen called the police and told them that Ricky and Jimmy were behind the Midway smoke shop and said that they were getting ready to take off to California. The whole police department swarmed around Midway, where they arrested Ricky and Jimmy.

Sandrine at party for her boyfriend Chuck Cheshire

And there was one more person the cops had to pick up: Albert lead Detective Gene.

Roma and Nancy Quinones have been friends for many years. Gene Roma called up Nancy Quinones and said, "We're looking for your son, Albert. Do you know where he is?"

My mother replied, "Why?"

Gene Rome said, "We just need to ask him a few questions."

Nancy replied, "I believe he's on the docks, fishing with his friends. Is everything all right, Jean?"

Gene Roma said, "We just need to ask him a few questions, and then I will bring him home. I promise."

Mark, Richie, and I were sitting on the docks when we heard sirens go off. We looked up and saw a string of cop cars coming down Main Street, heading toward us at the docks. I said to the guys, "Remember, I didn't tell you guys anything for a reason. It's because I don't want them to interrogate you. Guys, I am sorry this happened. Just tell them the truth. You don't know anything because they're going to separate us."

They had helicopters flying above us. The cops were driving down Main Street and drove right up onto the docks to block the dock off, and they started running down the docks with their guns drawn out, telling us to put our hands up. They grabbed each of us one by one, separated us, put us in different cars, and drove us back to the Northport police station to begin interrogating us. And they wanted to know what was said and what happened. They began to release everyone one by one except for me. They kept asking me and repeatedly what happened that night to Gary. I said I didn't know what they were talking about. After everything I had been through—the trauma of losing two friends and being beaten by the police officers for four and a half hours—I still hadn't told them anything.

The DA from the Suffolk County court district was in the Northport police station. I had no idea that Ricky and Jimmy Troiano had already been picked up and placed in two separate rooms. Ricky and Jimmy were questioned. Jimmy, within five seconds, ratted and was trying to cut a deal with the DA. The district attorney didn't like Jimmy because of his long criminal history. The DA didn't want to even hear anything Jimmy had to say.

Jean Roma and the DA walked into the room that I was in. The DA introduced himself to me and said, "We know everything. We know you have nothing to do with it, Albert. If we bring Ricky Kasso into the room and he tells you to tell us everything, will you tell us everything, then?"

I then did not believe it, but I agreed to do so only if I heard it from Ricky's mouth. Jean Romer went into the other room and brought Ricky into my room.

Ricky said to me, "I told to them everything and that you had nothing to do with it, and I'm sorry, Albert, for what happened. And tell your mother that I'm sorry and that I never meant to hurt her and never meant for this to happen."

Jean Roma then walked Ricky Kasso out of the room.

They made a deal with me for immunity and said I would go home but and only if I gave a statement that made Jimmy an accomplice. The DA was out to get Jimmy; they did not like Jimmy, and cops wanted to get Jimmy any way they could.

The rumor was that Jimmy had stolen the DA's car at gunpoint before they went upstate. The DA said to me, "If you don't make Jimmy an accomplice and take the immunity, then we're going to make both of you accomplices and put you both in jail, and this is the statement you have to sign. Then we'll let you go home right now with immunity."

I was so confused and didn't know what to do, and I was also scared. I looked over at Gene Romo, the police-officer friend of the family.

Officer Roma than said to me, "Just sign it. I'll take you home, I promise."

Then I looked at Officer Roma again and signed the papers, not feeling good about lying. The reporters were all over the police station. Officer Roma walked me out to his car and drove me to my house. The reporters were all over my house as Gene pulled up to the house, walked me up to my mother's door, and told her that I was involved in a murder but had nothing to do with it. Gene also told her I was a witness and that the DA gave me immunity to be the witness for the district attorney. My mother was in complete shock. She failed to keep me out of trouble gain.

The chief of police, Howie, made a statement saying that it was a cult, not realizing the guy that dug up the grave, Randy Guther, was already arrested for robbing the Indian graveyard in Northport. Howie then tried to retract the statement to the media but was too late; the media was not about to listen to any retractions the chief of police had made. They were making their money hand over fist and not caring if it was true or not, whether they were destroying more families. And me having to have seen my best friend murdered by his best friend. Shortly after that, I was torn away from my friends. I was being forced to lie by the DA. I'd been beaten up for four and a half hours, not knowing what to do, or who I could trust.

Rolling Stone came over to my friend Rich Barton's house. I figured that maybe I could tell my side of the story and that if I told the truth, everything would be all right. So I started walking across the street, and when I got to the house to sit down to talk to *Rolling Stone*, my mother had walked right into Sally Barton's house and stopped me from doing any interview. She took me back home, called the DA, and told them that *Rolling Stone* was trying to get an interview but that she stopped the interview. And *Rolling Stone* was mad because they couldn't get the interview that they wanted from me. So the interview never took place.

Later on, I told my mother I was sorry. I just did not want to lie in court, and they were forcing me to. My only chance to get the truth out there was pulled away from me within fifteen seconds. The DA, William Keaton, was coaching me for weeks on a lie; he wanted me to hang Jimmy. I did not feel comfortable with doing that to Jimmy.

I said to the DA; I didn't feel comfortable with lying in court.

The DA said, "That's the only way you'll get an immunity, Albert, or you both will go to jail. You will do what I tell you to do, Albert."

When the trial came along, it felt like it was forever. I was called to the stand. The pressure and stress were all on me. All eyes were on me. The whole world was watching me and waiting to see what I was going to say.

Jimmy was sitting across me, scared and not knowing what I was going to say. His life was in my hands. My friend Ricky just hung himself in jail under a twenty-four-hour suicide watch. How was it possible when police officers were watching him? So many things were running through my head. I was trying to process what happened to Ricky, Jimmy, and Gary and wondered what would happen if I told the lie the DA wanted me to say. I kept thinking about Ricky Kasso in jail. If Ricky Kasso was under the twenty-four-hour suicide watch, how was it that he was able to hang himself? The cops were supposed to be watching Ricky Kasso in the Riverhead jail around the clock. How was Ricky Kasso able to write graffiti all over his cell when he was being watched by the police around the clock? Would they have stopped him from writing graffiti all over his cell? It made no sense to me.

I started to think that the police had more to do with it than what they were saying, but no one ever spoke about it. They left it as if it never happened. I was thinking that I'd be the next one on the cops hit list and Jimmy too. I had to worry about one thing: whether I was going to hang an innocent man or not or if Jimmy was really at fault.

For Gary and Ricky's death, I have to live with that for the rest of my life. Now the DA was trying to get me to hang Jimmy Troiano, and I believe the DA was trying to set me up as well and hit me with perjury. If I told the DA's story, then they would have both of us in jail. I had to make a quick decision. Should I go with the DA's lies, or should I just tell the truth and hope for the best? There was not much time left. I had to go on the stand within minutes. The fate of Jimmy's life depended on my decision. As much as I did not like Jimmy and the problems that Jimmy caused within a month that Jimmy had been in Northport, I had to be fair about his decision.

I had an attorney, and his name was Richard Liberty. He was sitting behind the district attorney, William Keaton, and listening to every illegal thing that the DA was trying to say and lie on the stand. Nobody knew that I had an attorney on the side that heard everything that was going on and saw everything that was going on (The author's comment: until now everybody knows who my lawyer was), and as I was going up to the stand, Richard Liberty, my attorney from Garden City, New York, told me (after hearing what Bill Keaton, district attorney, said) on the down low told Albert to tell them the truth and not lie. He whispered that to me as I was walking to the stand.

I got up, walked over to the stand, and sat down in the chair. I looked over at Richard Labrant, my private lawyer, who nodded his head again and whispered, "Tell the truth, Albert." Then I looked over at the DA.

I was scared and took a deep breath, then I started to give my statement. I told the truth. The DA was in total shock that I didn't stay with the DA's story.

The judge stopped me and said, "This is not the statement you gave the DA and the police."

I replied to the judge, saying, "I know, Your Honor, but the DA wanted me to lie to put Jimmy Troiano in jail. And I can't live with putting an innocent man in jail for something he didn't do." I apologized to the judge, then everyone looked at me in shock. The whole courtroom was in silence.

Then the judge look at William Keaton and asked him, "Is this true?"

The DA from Suffer county court district was at a loss for words and had nothing to say, then the judge turned to me and said, "It takes a brave man to go through what you went through and to be able to go on the stand and tell us the truth. Thank you, Albert. We'll take a break for thirty minutes now." The judge called the DA and Naiburg to go to his chambers.

The trial lasted for about eight weeks. They continued to question me on everything. It was as if they were trying to get me to slip up, but my story stayed consistent because it was the truth. I did not understand why the trial lasted as long as it did; if his statement exonerated the defendant, it should've ended that day. Jimmy and I were never arrested, and I have never been arrested for anything. From what my lawyer, Richard Labert, told me, they were trying to screw me and get two birds with one stone to create a media circus.

I remember lying on my grandmother's lap when I was a kid, and my grandmother always said, "Albert, if you have a nightmare, write it in the book, and after a week, take all your nightmares and throw them away." But it seems that my nightmares became reality and keep getting worse with the fake media and author.

MY FINAL YEARS OF SCHOOL

When the trial was over, I had to make a decision. My grandmother always said to me, "Without an education, Albert, you will go nowhere in life." My mother forced that and instilled that into my life too. I was upset, hurt, and traumatized, but I knew I couldn't stay in Northport and get the education that

I needed to get on with my life; not with the media circus and reporters camping outside my house and chasing everyone down for interviews. My mother and I sat down and spoke, and we came to the decision that it would be better if I went out of state for school—as if this wasn't enough for me; I lost my two best friends. I was fifteen years old and ripped apart by the media. I was forced to stay away from my friends. Basically, I was isolated in my room by myself, and no one talked to because no one in my family wanted to talk about it. My mother had good friends—Linda and Dave Darty. My mother asked Linda if it would be all right for if I could stay with them, and she said, "Most certainly. Albert is a good kid." Linda said to my mother, "Nancy, I'm sorry this happened to your family. Albert used to go to church with us and our kids in Upper Room Tabernacle in Deer Park. I cannot believe this happened to your family. Dave and I will do whatever It takes to help you, Nancy and Albert. My husband David and I have a church in Griffin, Georgia, and a house about forty-five minutes outside Atlanta Georgia with an extra bedroom, and if Albert wants to fly out there next week, Albert can. But he must go to school there."

Nancy replied to Linda, "Thank you so much, Linda. I don't know what I would do without you, Linda."

"Nancy, we have been friends our whole life and went to school together. Friends are supposed to help each other out, Nancy. We love you guys. You work hard, and it's not easy raising three kids on your own, Nancy."

"I will be the one to tell Albert that he must leave next week, and I will call you, Linda, when and what time Albert will be there."

Linda replied to Nancy, "David and I will pick Albert up at the airport. Just let us know the date and time." Mom then got off the phone with Linda.

I was standing in the hallway, and I heard my mom talking to Linda. I was hurt. I felt like everyone was just trying to get rid of me. I knew I made a mistake, being at the wrong place at the wrong time.

My mom said, "Albert, I need to talk to you."

I came out of the hallway and went to the kitchen. I said, "I know, Mom. I understand." I told her I'd get my things ready for next week.

"Albert, it's for your own good. It's too crazy here with the reporters and everyone else. You've been through enough, Albert. I want you to know we love you."

I said, "I know." I turned around and went back to my bedroom. I was hurt because I'd always been there to protect my sister and my mother. I felt unwanted and all alone. I was also confused, but I didn't want to be a burden to them. Deep down inside, I wanted to die.

I had no one to turn to. I was not allowed to talk to my friends and was not allowed out of the house. I was isolated from the world like I had the black plague.

My mother had disowned her side of the family as well as her husband's side of the family. For her own reasons, Nancy did not speak to either side when growing up as a kid. My mother and sisters didn't want to talk about the murder that Ricky Kasso committed. I felt like they resented me.

The following weekend, I had to get ready to leave to go to Georgia. Mom and my sisters Wendy and Debbie just told me they loved me and said everything would be all right, but inside, I felt they resented me and didn't believe they were telling the truth. But it's okay. I know I messed it up, and I have to own it and take whatever repercussions it had. But it became very tiring mentally and physically for me.

At the age of sixteen years old, it was clear to me: I knew I was all alone, and I had to take control of the situation. I knew that whatever chances I had in getting a scholarship and going to college were all gone now, but I knew I had to finish school. One way or another, I had to graduate school.

It was a sunny day out, and a lot of tension was in the air. Mom said she was going to get the car to take me to the airport and that there was a reporter outside, and she told me not to speak to the reporter and that she would honk the horn for me to come out.

"I know, Mom. I've been doing this for a long time and long enough to know the drill now."

My mom pulled the car up to the front of the house and beeped the horn. I started walking to the car with my bags. The reporter got in my face, started taking pictures, and was trying to get a statement from me. I was so pissed off that I smacked the camera out of the reporter's hand and pushed the reporter out of the way. I told the reporter he was trespassing and that if he didn't get away from my house, or I would beat the reporter's ass into oblivion. The reporter laughed and said, "I have more shit right about you, Albert."

The reporter started to laugh at me again. It was a game to the reporters; they were doing whatever they could to just try to get some more shit on me in the papers just to make money.

When I got to the car, my mother got mad at me. She said, "I told you not to talk to them."

I got into the car, put my head down, and said, "I am sorry, Mom."

It seemed like that was all I ever did—apologize for everything and nothing. As we drove off, there was silence all the way to the airport. After we arrived at John F. Kennedy International Airport and pulled in front of the TWA terminal, I got out of the car and started grabbing my bags.

My mother got out of the car and said, "Albert, I love you, but this is for your own good. I know if you stay here, you're gonna end up hurting someone, and you're going to get locked up. And that's what they're trying to do to you, Albert."

"I know, Mom. I know. I'm sorry. I'll give you a call when I get to Georgia. I love you too. Mom."

I walked into the terminal, went to the TWA terminal, and gave them my ID. I then checked my bags in and grabbed my ticket.

I sat down, waiting for my airplane outside gate 22. And then the tears started coming down my eyes. Everything came tumbling down. I lost two of my best friends. They were dead, and I was not allowed to talk to the friends I grew up with. I lost all my scholarships and had to leave my home at sixteen years of age. I wondered if it could get any worse than that. I was all alone now more than ever.

I went to the bathroom because I didn't want anyone to see that I was upset, and that's when I really broke down. I stayed in the bathroom for twenty minutes, trying to get myself together before I left the bathroom. I cried so much that there were no more tears. I threw water on my face and pulled myself together. I had $100 in my pocket, I lost everyone I cared for, and I had to start over at sixteen years old. I didn't want the money because I felt like I didn't earn it, but I appreciated it. My plane was going to be there in ten minutes. I grabbed a soda and some potato chips before I boarded the plane.

I was so tired that I fell asleep on the plane, and before I knew it, I was in the terminal in Atlanta, Georgia. It was about a four-hour flight. I went to the luggage claim and went outside to wait. It was a nice sunny day out. I felt like a weight was lifted off my back for some reason.

Linda and David came to the airport and picked me up in a gray van. Linda's husband, David, got out of the van to help me put my luggage in the back of the van. As they were driving back to their house, Linda and her husband, David, were playing gospel music, and only thing I could think of was that this was not gonna work. I believed in God, but this was getting a little over the top for me at this time.

Linda and David asked me how I was doing. I replied that I was doing fine.

I was destroyed. I was scared to say anything because I didn't know if I was going to say the right thing or the wrong thing, and I didn't want them to be mad at me. So I stayed quiet.

David said, "Albert, you are going to be fine. You'll get through this, Albert."

As we pulled up to Linda and David's house, Linda got out of the van, put her arms around me, and said, "Albert, you're gonna be fine," and she started walking me to the house.

Linda brought me to the house, walked me down the hallway to the spare room, and told me to unpack and that we were having dinner at 4:00 PM. Linda said, "Albert, if you want to rest, you can, but you have no choice but to be at the table for dinner, and whoever doesn't show up for dinner doesn't eat until the next day."

But I was okay with that because, and I was happy I had a roof over my head and no reporters harassing me.

I felt as if some of the stress was off me, and no one knew where I was. But I missed my friends because they were there as a good support group. We spoke about everything. We helped one another out. That was all taken away.

Linda's husband, David, was a preacher. They had their own church. Linda and David wanted to make sure that we all knew the house rules and that we obeyed them. We went to church three times a week—Sunday, Wednesday, and Friday. Linda's husband was the preacher, so when he went to church, we went to church. House rule number 2 was that after dinner, you had to clean up after yourself, wash your own dishes. and put them away. House rule number three: We should take twenty-minute showers and clean the shower when you are finished for the next person.

I knew that David was going to say something about my cigarettes. He could smell the smoke on me and he had a nose like a hound dog. I was waiting for this because I was not about to stop smoking cigarettes. It was the only thing I had left.

David was six feet four inches tall and about 250 pounds, and he scared the shit out of me and would've eaten me like a cookie. David said, "Albert, I smell cigarette smoke on you, so if you go to smoke, do it in the backyard and put the butts in the can." That was one of my happiest moments. I was in shock. He didn't take the only thing I enjoyed away from me. He winked at me.

I replied, "Yes, sir," with respect. These rules were all new to me. I was not used to having someone enforcing rules. Everyone must be up at 5:00 AM, eat, and be at the school bus stop at seven. These rules—all the rules—were new to me, but I would obey them.

*****

It was the first day of school. I was scared but made a lot of friends. All the girls liked me because I was from New York. The guys were jealous of me since I was a big hit. I was reborn again in church in September 1985 at the Central Lake Church of God in Griffin, Georgia.

I became very deep in spirituality and started talking in tongues. That's when I knew God had a purpose for me. Because if he did not, I would never have been blessed with the language of tongues. It's a language that communicates from the spirit of God and to this day, I still talk in tongues.

As time went on, the school year was coming to an end. Linda andher husband David started fighting a lot. I think it was about bills and finances. It made me feel uncomfortable. Then I got a job working at a restaurant—specifically, I was prepping food at a restaurant—and was going to school. I was putting my money away, then I thanked Linda and Dave. I told them I had a friend whose father was a WWF wrestler, very well-known and famous, and I was going to move in with him by the school, which was also close to my job. Shortly after that, I moved in with Jason, and we went to his father's house. I saw his father, and he gave us a ride on his plane, which he had in the barn in the backyard. And he showed me all of his belts and trophies. I was somewhat jealous of him because he had a father and I didn't, but I was happy that I had his friendship.

His father took me in like one of his own kids. His dad would take us fishing and hiking. His dad took us to the Grand Canyon, the Indian reservations, Hoover Dam, and the redwood forest. I was blessed to have him as a friend, and if he's reading this, I want him to know I was blessed to have him and his father in my life. I'm grateful. Thank you, big chief.

The school year was out, and I had one year left to go. I made plans to go back to New York and told Jason, "Thank you and your father for being there for me. I am going back to New York."

Jason replied, "If you need me, Albert, I'll always be here for you." He said, "If it gets too hard, Albert, you need to get out of Northport. Call me my father, and I will be more than happy to take you back any time, Albert."

I replied to Jason, "Thank you very much, but I'll be fine."

"You're a good soul, Albert. Just know that," Jason said. "Well, if you're gonna leave me, Albert, and go back to New York, we might as well get drunk and get some girls." Jason started laughing.

Albert replied, "Let's do it. Rock it out, buddy boy. We got this." as I started to laugh with my friend.

We drank, and hung out with some girls from school, it was the first party I had growing up as a kid. And I had a great time. It was a farewell party. And most of the girls from my school came over. The guys were jealous. They didn't really care too much for anyone from New York.

I flew back to New York, and my mother picked me up at the airport. She asked me how I was doing. I replied to my mother and told her I was doing fine. But really, I felt the stress all over again. I felt as if I was going to say the wrong thing. I didn't feel wanted all over again and wanted to leave and go back to Georgia.

At sixteen years old, I knew I couldn't run from my problems. I had to face it head-on—the only way to fix the problem. I got back to my house, and as soon I got home, I called up Richie Barton. I saw that my friends went through a lot of shit with the reporters. It was like the paparazzi gave them hell. We were all glad to be together again; that was our happy place—being together. Rumor has it that Jimmy supposedly went back to Albany, and no one really cared where Jimmy went. We were glad because we didn't want him around us. Jimmy was bad news from the beginning. Jimmy was jealous of all of us because we were so close like family, and Jimmy didn't have that in his life. Jimmy Troiano was an adopted child with a lot of issues, anger, and jealousy. Of all of us, Jimmy was the downfall of Northport. Jimmy tried to create this nightmare for all of us, and then he ran back, pointing his finger and laughing at all of us. Jimmy Troiano was an evil, rotten soul.

So this is my story. It was two friends whom I cared for like brothers.

EYEWITNESS

Albert graduated from Northport High School in June 1986. It was his prom day.

Albert was excited that his life was going to have a new beginning

Albert ordered a limousine for him and his girlfriend, Sharon Johnson from Kings Park.

Sharon Johnson was a beautiful girl with long blonde hair and blue eyes—very slim with a perfect body shape.

Albert's plans were to pick Sharon Johnson up at her house. Then they would go into Manhattan to Tavern on the Green to meet up with his friends for dinner and then head into New Jersey to spend the night at the Holiday Inn Hotel and go to the great adventure of Six Flags in the morning.

The limo was on its way to Albert's house on 85 Maple Avenue when the call came in from the limo company, saying that the limo broke down.

Albert was in shock, but the limo company, Thomas, asked Albert if he wanted a Rolls-Royce instead at no extra charge.

Albert was excited and accepted the Rolls-Royce.

Albert couldn't wait to surprise his girlfriend with a Rolls-Royce.

ALBERT QUINONES

Albert picked her up. Sharon was surprised and very happy.

Albert's mother wanted Albert to come to Eatons Neck to her work, so Albert's mom could get photos of Albert and Sharon because it was a nice place to take photos.

As the Rolls-Royce went down to Eatons Neck to Albert's mothers job and pulled into the driveway, Albert and Sharon Johnson got out of the Rolls-Royce his mother, Nancy.

She introduced that man to Albert as Roy Block, her boyfriend.

Albert was in complete shock and had no idea that his mother was dating someone

Albert was somewhat mad because his mother was never around, and now he realized why she was never around.

As time went on, Albert realized that man was not Roy Block.

That man's name was David St Claire: the man who wrote the book called *Say You Love Satan in the Suburbs*—the book that tarnished Albert's image, the book that destroyed Albert's life, and the reason why

Nancy Quinones hasn't spoken to him in over three years for writing this book.

To be continued.

CONCLUSION
LOOKING BACK

1) There are so many inaccuracies about what happened that night in 1984.
2) Every year, it seems like there's a new documentary or book or movie.
3) I was there, and I've lived with this every single day.
4) The real lesson is children need to be watched and kept in check.
5) I hope my coming forward will help bring closure to people like Gary's parents, who've struggled with this situation for so long.

6) I witnessed this, and I live with the pain in the nightmares and heartache of the loss of my two best friends every day.

The people in this book had someway shape or form or involvement in my story. They interviewed with me and only me.

Conducted interviews are researched and recorded and written by the author.

- Albert Quinones—wrong place at the wrong time
- Rich Barton—went to see the grave of Gary Lauwers
- Mark Florimonte—witnessed Albert being picked up by police
- Randy Guthler—confessed that he dug up the Indian graveyard with no one else
- William Billy Leason—the one who lied for his name in fame
- Robert Atkinson—next-door neighbor friend of the Quinones family
- Sara Gatto—Ricky Kasso's girlfriend
- Karen Novollino—Jimmy Troiano's girlfriend

- Gene Roemer—lead detective and a longtime friend of the Quinones family
- Lori Walsh—her father is a police officer at Northport, and she did the right thing
- Debbie Quinones—Gary Lauwers's girlfriend
- Richard Libert—private attorney of Albert Quinones
- Philip Morelli—everyone's friend

I want to thank my friends who gave me the interviews and waited for me to do this book thirty-eight years. If it wasn't for them and their help, the book would not be as good as it is. And thank you for your support.

I don't know if Jimmy manipulated or influenced Ricky to kill Gary. Only God will know and be able to judge him.

Jimmy Triano did not hold Gary Lauwers down, give Ricky Kasso the knife, or help Ricky.

Ricky Kasso took full responsibility for his crime. The acid king book was the beginning of destroying my life again. I lost my job, I lost my pension, I lost my girlfriend, and lost my apartment.

I was no more than a witness. I live with the pain and scars of losing my two best friends. I am reliving the nightmare and pain to write this book and to give everyone the closure they need to move on in their lives.

Thank you Jesse P. Pollick for destroying my life again. Not getting the story straight, your interviewing, or the correct people. You have the book of lies. You should be ashamed of yourself for doing what you did to these people and me, so let God judge you for your crime.

SOURCES

Breskin, D. "Cult Killing: Kids in the Dark." *Rolling Stone*, November 18, 2019. https://www.rollingstone.com/culture/culture-features/long-island-devil-cult-murder-ricky-kasso-david-breskin-901069/.

Hornblower, M. "Youths' Deaths Tied to Satanic Rite." *Washington Post*, July 1984. https://www.washingtonpost.com/archive/politics/1984/07/09/youths-deaths-tied-to-satanic-rite/3286f188-2636-4dbf-a6eb-9b767f1adb5c/.

sataninthesuburbs. "Satan in the Suburbs—Interview with Jimmy Troiano." YouTube, June 2008. https://www.youtube.com/watch?v=uHjK8rJ83cw.

ACKNOWLEDGMENTS

THE AUTHOR WISHES to sincerely thank the following people who helped make this possible:

Frank Visconte	William Lesson	James Lamb	Ronnie CarAntonio
Killer Tony from Harlem New York	Jennifer Maisie	Richie Gambino	Dorothy Jacobson
Frank Piscotty	Kasso family Peggy Giuliani	Beverly Bruno Heidi Bruno	Kerry Condon
Philip Morel	Bobby Bruno	Steven and Floyd Sarisohn Motor Parkway Smithtown, NY	Alyssa McGinnis from Newman Springs Publishing
Randy Guther	My friend breeze	Adem Kameraj	Lizabeth from Newman Springs Publishing
Mark Florimonte	Richard Laberty— Contract Lawyer, Garden City, NY	Gary's family	James Gordon from Newman Springs Publishing

John Giuliani	Karen Naveliono	Karen Avelino	Michele Weinberg from Newman Springs Publishing
Richie Palme	Richard Barton	Gene Romer (Northport police)	Anthony Garcia from Newman Springs Publishing
Cindy from gates Denise de Salvatore	Richard Liberty (lawyer from 1984)	Robert Atkinson	
Laurie Walsh	Nancy Martinez	Vinny Ferrara	
Roxanne from West Germany	Laura Wash	Ronnie CarAntonio	
Johnny Pierpont			

And first and most of all, Elizabeth, my all.

ABOUT THE AUTHOR

ALBERT WAS BORN in Smithtown, New York. Albert Quinones graduated from Northport High School, class of 1986. Albert put hours into enlisting him-self in the United States army as a combat engineer from 1986. He received an honorable discharge in 1994 and received an army achievement medal. The excellent perform passed down from president George Bush. Then he went to Briar Cliff college as a computer, networker, and programmer then ran a repair shop at Meineke in Queens, New York. Albert Quinones moved on to being one of the carpenters in the 1556 labor union as a shop steward. Albert Quinones eventually went on to having his own construction company: Five Boroughs Construction Group.

www.ingramcontent.com/pod-product-compliance
Lightning Source LLC
Chambersburg PA
CBHW020352170426
43200CB00005B/142